For Sis and Billy

Billy, over the holi[days]
your <u>Reflections</u>,
it is truly inspiring!
These anecdotes are just light reading,
but I had fun writing them. Enjoy.

It Begins It Ends
It Ends It Begins

Love to
You both,
Judy

PS I remember as if it were yesterday,
riding past McCaskin's cottage and
stopping to listen to you practicing on
your violin! You were already a
Renaissance Man!

It Begins It Ends
It Ends It Begins

Judy Richter

Copyright © 2011 by Judy Richter.

Library of Congress Control Number: 2011919487
ISBN: Hardcover   978-1-4653-8948-0
               Softcover   978-1-4653-8947-3
               Ebook   978-1-4653-0551-0

All rights reserved. No part of this book may be reproduced or transmitted in any form or by any means, electronic or mechanical, including photocopying, recording, or by any information storage and retrieval system, without permission in writing from the copyright owner.

This book was printed in the United States of America.

To order additional copies of this book, contact:
Xlibris Corporation
1-888-795-4274
www.Xlibris.com
Orders@Xlibris.com
103343

CONTENTS

Foreword: Henry Webb 11
Preface: 15
Introduction: Looking Back . . . And Ahead 19

I. Histories 21
    Max's Baumkuchen 23
    Letter to Max 27
    FHCDS in the Fifties 31
    Dogs I Have Slept With 35
    My Two Favorite Fleabags 39
    Our Neighbor's Woods and Fields 42
    Block Island 46
    Peri Wahn: Then and Now 48
    An Evocative Object: My Saddle 55
    Sixty Years at the Devon Horse Show 58

II. Horses 71
    Gypsy 73
    Who is Lady Ardmore Anyway? 79
    Who is Stacey? What is She? 85
    Queenie and the Circle of Life 89
    Just for Fun: His Induction into the National Hall of Fame 92
    Glasgow: A Great Horse 94
    Blink: A Keeper 97

III. The West 101
    A Ride on a Cutting Horse 103
    Wyoming: 107
        Prologue 107
        Wrangling at the 7D Ranch 108
        A Horse With A Flying Tail 115
    Mentors and Protégés: Handing Over the Reins 117

IV. Minutiae On and Off the Farm 121
    Nail Polish 123
    Tiny Triumphs 124
    On Sleeping Outside 128
    Multiple Miracles: Popcorn Pups 130
    The Mouse and Nurse Diesel 133
    Vermont Mice 135
    My New Thermos 137
    My New Lawnmower 139
    Learning Styles at the Horse Gym 141
    The Pulley Rein 144
    The Beaver Dam 148
    A Proposed Swarm 150
    Is You Family? 152

V. Paintings, Prints, Portraits, Photos 155
    Thomas Oldaker: Nineteenth Century Huntsman and
    Family Friend 157
    "Ex Libris": More Keepers 160
    A Family of Foxhunters 163
    A Treasured Painting 167
    Three Offers Comes to Coker Farm 172

VI. Adventures Off the Farm 177
    Still No Offers 179
    Willard at Saratoga 182
    Racing Our Car 183
    Riding in the Maryland Hunt Cup 185
    John Kingery: Big Owner at the Quarter Horse World
    Championships 186
    West Palm Beach: The Ups and Downs of Show Jumping 188

VII. Road Trips 191
    Roads Often Taken 193
    Columbus Day Weekend 199
    Our Trip to Lagrangeville 203
    "Go West, Young Man, Go West" 209

For My Family

Hans and Jennifer, Maxine and Margot

Philip and Sarah

And My Friend

Nicholas Snow Maher

Epigraph:

Carpe diem

Horace

If there is a sin against life, it consists perhaps not so much in despairing of life as in hoping for another life and in eluding the implacable grandeur of this life.

Albert Camus (1913-1960)

Foreword

Nothing can prepare you for the charm, adventure and beauty of Judy Richter's work, so I won't try. In this, her second volume of reminiscences, we encounter a modern-day pioneer, an equestrian and farmer whose lifestyle spans centuries. She takes her calls on her iPhone during her morning ride through the hills of northern Westchester, or between training students at a horse show in West Palm Beach or just sitting on her back patio overlooking a field of grazing horses, with wooded hills in the distance.

Judy is a horse trader, an occupation going back, not centuries, but eons. It has a romantic ring to it, horse trader, but it also brings to mind sly dealings, if not outright thievery. Judy is a hard bargainer, but she is no thief. You quickly realize that you are in the hands of someone you can trust, a reliable expert who knows man and beast, someone earthy and sophisticated, with a sharp eye for both the beautiful and the absurd. No, she won't cheat you, but she may inadvertently steal your heart.

Like many horse traders Judy has traveled far and wide, to Europe and Ireland and the mountains of Wyoming. True to her kinship with her ancient forebears she has brought back not only horses, but tales to tell, which she does in a lucid, conversational voice, that laid back talk around the kitchen table tone that seems so easy, so deceptively easy. One of her favorite poets is Robert Frost, and her voice may remind you of his. It is the voice of one who cares for the land, for whom the weather is more than a matter of convenience, who knows that the day's tasks cannot be ignored.

Central to Judy's stories are two intertwined, inseparable roots, the deep attachments that ground her: her family and her farm. She and her husband of over four decades began their life together in a walk-up in New York City. But riding horses was a focus for both of them, and the country beckoned. So when the opportunity presented itself, they moved. Judy was at the time an English teacher, no surprise there, and her husband was a young, German emigrant who came here to live the American dream. They found each other, raised two boys, now very capable men, and with daring, hard work, and mutual support, accomplished their dreams.

Max, who died in 2007, built a successful paper business, and together they bought the farm, Coker Farm, the delights, beauty and demands of which you will encounter as you read. These enterprises weren't achieved without risk. So one wonderful piece of this story is the marriage of two bright, active people with very defined personal goals who buoyed and supported each other through thick and thin.

As I said, Judy started her career as a teacher and a teacher she remains. The venue just shifted a bit, from the classroom to the jumps. She rides well; she would never assert that herself, but there's a shelf of trophies and ribbons that speak for her. She has also written several books on training horses and riders: *Riding for Kids, Horse and Rider, Longeing,* and *Pony Talk* that speak even louder.

When it comes to "showing" horses, you mustn't imagine an animal being pranced out there to be admired for its breeding and conformation. For Judy and her peers, it means that a horse and its rider are completing a course of jumps, obstacles that demand skill, precision, courage and presence of mind. It is a dangerous sport, and though horsemen don't talk about it much, each time they go out, both horse and rider could, well, "come a cropper." Yet there is nothing more exhilarating than testing yourself to the full in a situation demanding the utmost grace under pressure.

Given that we are speaking of a highly skilled endeavor, clearly those horsemen (men and women) weren't born with those skills and, furthermore, those horses didn't just happen to be able to jump those incredible fences with ease and elegance, pacing themselves to leap the next one. Both horse and rider require a certain temperament and the physical endowments to go forward, but that's only where it begins. They must then both be trained. And that is what Judy has done most of her working life; she has trained horse and rider to compete.

Often Judy will say something like, "What I try to do is teach riders to stay out of the way of their horses." What she means and sometimes says explicitly is that horse and rider must develop an intuitive understanding of each other, so close that they are at all times acting as a single unit, not unlike the fabled centaur. To train these animals, man and beast, the teacher must herself be an astute observer of both. In this case we not only have such a teacher, we also have an articulate writer who can tell us stories of the process. The horses are as present as their riders, good natured or cranky, big and small, bold or skittish.

She is also an adventurer, someone who quickens with the chase, a woman who went off riding hell-for-leather in the Wyoming wilderness rounding up stray horses, earning the (one can be sure) grudging respect of a bunch of seasoned cowboys who might have just had the uneasy feeling she could ride rings around them. She's never easy to pin down, least of all when she's in the saddle.

Underlying many of Judy's pieces, giving them a weight that is both informative and compelling, is an awareness of the inevitable movement of time. Life brings us great joy, then takes it away, has its compensations, great losses, marvelous gains. We must endure as well as appreciate. We find ways to go on.

So here is Judy Richter, dear reader. Her prose is lucid, her stories entertain, and the depth of feeling she offers is restorative. Go with her into that lovely spread called Coker Farm. In his foreword to Judy's first book of reminiscences, *Some Favorite Days*, Steven Schnur asks,

> What is it like to spend a lifetime living and working among horses and those devoted to their care? What does it mean to own a farm an hour north of Manhattan and to move continuously between the parallel worlds of that frenetic city and rural Bedford? How does it feel to prepare for world-class competition, to travel the world in search of promising horses, to trade, to groom, to transport, even to bury, beloved four-legged friends, to endure disappointment and elation and the day-to-day drama of raising a family on a farm?

Turn the page.

Henry Webb
Croton-on-Hudson, N.Y.

Preface:

Though leaves are many, the root is one;
Through all the lying days of my youth
I swayed my leaves and flowers in the sun;
Now I may wither into truth.

W.B. Yeats

I may, or I may not, "wither into truth." That is a lofty goal, perhaps too lofty for me. Daunting is my task to depict the interesting and wonderful people and horses, events and venues that continue to brighten my days. My human and equine friends encourage me to look ahead with as much enthusiasm and optimism as I look behind with nostalgia and gratitude for my good life.

As for the writing about my experiences, colleagues in my writing class at Sarah Lawrence College and the Greenwich Pen Women, a group of published writers, steadfastly endorse my efforts to describe the comings and goings on and off the farm. For nearly two decades I have studied under Steve Schnur's tutelage at Sarah Lawrence, enjoying his guidance and encouragement. Classmates, notably Hank Webb, spur me on to write more . . . and better. My two pen pals, Emory Clark and Peter Green, have been staunch supporters for years. We still communicate by snail mail. Without my tireless typist, Kathy Farina, my arduous proofreader, Anne Sullivan, and Eleanor Honig, who organized the photographs, none of this would have seen the light of day. Writing these pieces has been fun and part of the fun is sharing them with you, with thanks to the encouragement and help from the above-mentioned and many others as well.

Prologue

It is now nearly five years since my husband, Max, died. Having known and loved him for over fifty years, I could not imagine life without him. Yet, for those of us left, life continues; it begins, it ends, it ends, it begins, and so it was for me, thanks to the support of family and friends: old and new, human, equine, and canine.

"Looking Back" by Suzanne Gail Richardson, 1984.
This horse is not just looking back; he is also
looking around, alert to what lies ahead.

Introduction:
Looking Back . . . And Ahead

As dawn slipped slowly but inexorably over the wooded hill beyond our farm, my eyes focused on the dark eye of the white horse in the painting beyond the foot of my bed. The white horse and the white background were not visible yet, so I knew I had a few minutes of grace before I had to get up.

The painting "Looking Back," which I watch take shape every day as the skies brighten, is of a white horse who has turned his head to look behind him. Soon I would see his alert, pricked ears and the lines of his expressive face. What exactly is his expression? Different on different days depending on my own outlook: curious? nostalgic? eager? anxious? Always engaged. Likewise, I look back on my own life, mostly grateful that it has been full of countless opportunities.

Now that the sun was up over the hill outside, I could see his gracefully curved neck and ample hindquarters that frame his piercing eye and sharp ears. His nose is hidden below his back. Recently I realized that if I ever collect and publish another group of sketches about my life on and off the farm, many of the pieces inside will be just that: "Looking Back" . . . and looking ahead.

Blessed with a sweetheart of a husband, Max, and two sons, Hans and Philip, who inherited his good disposition, I enjoyed a peaceful, happy family life for nearly fifty years. My chosen profession, the horse business, enabled me "to unite/my avocation and my vocation/ as my two eyes make one in sight." (Robert Frost, "Two Tramps in Mud-Time")

In the years since Max's death from Alzheimer's complications, I have come to realize that Faulkner was right: "The past is not dead, it is not even past." Memories of our life together greet me often and encourage me to seek out the new. My life is as good as it can be without Max, thanks to family and friends, horses and dogs, my two farms in Bedford, New York, and East Barnard, Vermont. New tenants and clients have enriched my life immeasurably, and I am glad to look forward to good beginnings. Unexpected sources of joy are some old acquaintances, now new friends, notably Nick Maher, who brightens my life. Having grown up in Vermont in the '40's and '50's on separate trap lines, as it were, we share a geographical past that also is "not even past." Now in our '70's we enjoy revisiting old trap lines and exploring new ones as well. I hope to enjoy these beginnings, to "carpe diem," to seize the good moments as they come my way.

I.

Histories

Max's Baumkuchen

German Baumkuchen (tree cakes) have been a tradition in our family at Christmastime since 1957 when Max, later to be my husband of forty-six years, brought his precious Baumkuchen under his arm to my family's annual Christmas dinner with friends and neighbors. He had already charmed me several weeks before over Thanksgiving when we met fox hunting. Because he was so enthusiastic about my beloved horse Coker, he won my heart despite his odd looks in borrowed riding togs. Even though his ears stuck out sideways under a too-large bowler, I was, to say the least, kindly disposed, for he was keen on my horse. Imagine my delight on Christmas when I saw how divinely good-looking he was without that bowler on his head. His kind, sparkling blue eyes and cheerful smile brightened our Christmas gathering and brightened my life forever after. Little did I know on that Christmas day that over the years we would discover that we loved the same people, animals, places, food—LIFE . . . over fifty years of life together.

None of us Americans that evening long ago had any idea how very precious Max's Baumkuchen was. We assumed he picked it up in one of the shops on 86th Street, in those days "German town" where virtually no other language was spoken. This cake was special, however; his mother had sent it, (surface mail, air mail was too expensive), all the way from his home in Hamburg, Germany. Though he is gone, Max's tradition still exists today; just before Thanksgiving every year I order Baumkuchen from the Konditorei Kreutzkamm in Munich. Before the World War II bombing the cakes were made in Dresden and are known as the Dresdener Baumkuchen. Tasting it each Christmas sparks my memory not unlike Proust's when he tasted his madeleine. In fact, the delicate flavors of these two beloved lemony treats suggest they are probably distant cousins.

Long ago as we crowded around the kitchen table, Max carefully unwrapped the tall, rectangular box. Inside were multiple layers of almost transparent glassine paper through which we could barely see the thin sugar glaze covering the tall, delicious-looking cylinder. Finally it was totally unwrapped and stood in splendor on the kitchen counter until after dinner. It did indeed look like a tree trunk.

As we carried the dinner plates out to the kitchen, Max carefully laid the cake on its side on the wooden cutting board.

"Now, I need a really sharp knife," he declared. We produced our best knife, which he tried carefully against his thumb. The son of a butcher, he was particular that knives be sharp. This one was clearly too dull. It hadn't been sharpened in years, if ever. My father rummaged around in his toolbox and produced a whetstone, perfect for the job. Every trade has its skills, and to the end of his days, Max could transform a knife that couldn't cut hot butter into a blade that would thin-slice any roast or cheese or cake. Slowly Max drew the whetstone along the knife blade, first on one side, then the other, testing it often against his thumb. After a couple of dozen strokes he was satisfied and ready to cut the cake which lay like a fallen tree on the wooden board.

We stood around the table impatiently watching Max slicing the cake as thin as communion wafers while he explained that the flavor was better if the pieces were not thick. As he worked, he told us that the cake batter was added layer by layer and it did indeed look like tree rings on the inside and a tree trunk on the outside. No wonder the cake was called "Baumkuchen."

The taste is a mixture of lemon, vanilla, and marzipan, a well-known German candy, also a delicacy. Unlike heavy German fruitcake, of which one bite or two was usually more than enough, the pile of thin slices always disappeared quickly every year, year after year.

And so for over five decades thereafter, we have preserved the Baumkuchen tradition: always ordered before Thanksgiving, received in mid-December with eager anticipation, and finally enjoyed Christmas day and after whenever the family got together. First we celebrated out in New Jersey at my parents' farm, and then after we were married, in our little New York apartment, then a succession of garage apartments in Greenwich, finally in our own home, a cottage in Greenwich, and lastly our dear farm in Bedford. In our last two homes are fireplaces where we can gather around a cozy, warm fire as we enjoy our Baumkuchen.

Now over fifty years later, I sliced this year's Baumkuchen slowly and carefully. Lacking Max's skill and sharp knife, I did my best, and it was okay. Seated around the fire in gleeful anticipation were my granddaughters,

Baumkuchen.
We tasted it first on Christmas, 1957
and have enjoyed it ever since.

Maxine and Margot, and my daughter-in-law, Jennifer. My son, Hans, was hard at work in the kitchen washing dishes, like his Dad always used to do. The girls have developed a taste for Baumkuchen over the years; it's not hard to do.

As I carved the precious Baumkuchen, shaped like a tree trunk and lying on its side next to many fairly thin slabs on our big, round, wooden cheeseboard, I resisted the temptation to repeat the story they all knew from years of retellings. We waited impatiently for our hard-working dishwashing Hans, now the Dad, alone in the kitchen, to join us at the fire in the living room and savor once again our beloved Baumkuchen.

A Letter to Max from Borstel: Summer 2010

All of this you know, but some members of the Richter family and others may not.

Yesterday we buried your mother at age 99 in the vast, sun-drenched forest/park, Oldsdorf Cemetery, next to your long-gone father. Today the sun is shining still and the birds are chirping merrily at Borstel, your beloved garden in dear old Hamburg.

When Ernsti, your brother, proudly showed me around the garden, resplendent with roses—all shades of red, pink, white, and orange—all gracefully bowing on laden stems toward us, he wondrously remarked,

"This has been the best year for roses. So many of them and blooming more beautifully than ever; a fine goodbye and send-off for Oma."

And indeed all over Hamburg the roses were blooming as never before. Presided over by a tall tree covered with white blossoms and surrounded by blue hydrangeas, yellow "raps," and countless, nameless other plants and flowers, the many rose bushes were center stage in the garden this week, even as they climbed up the walls of the house and the encircling fence.

The garden has been in the family for generations, first Oma's, now ours. I remember meeting her mother, also "Oma," in 1960. She lived in a tiny cottage at the far end of the garden, built after the war, World War II, when the house and the butcher shop in front on the street were bombed out. Only rubble remained. Black and white photos of those days show the debris neatly swept in piles along the sidewalk. A few treasures they had the foresight to bury in the ground remained safely there until after the war was over: some silver and Pappi's precious Leica camera that still works perfectly today though its leather case is old and cracked. All their worldly possessions vanished into the rubble, but for Pappi, your father, the greatest loss was all the photos of you as children. He mourned that loss to the day he died, while he heroically rebuilt his life and his business.

Throughout the war and after, the gardens sustained your family and friends with vegetables of all sorts, planted in the spring, and canned to be eaten in the winter along with meat from Pappi's displaced and reactivated butcher shop. Hence you were not as hungry as most in those dismal, dark, post-war years.

After the war, there was frequent talk of selling the garden to jump start the business and provide money to live on. Somehow your parents scraped by, helped somewhat by the sale of your beloved summer cottage by the sea in Heilingenhafen.

As your parents aged and your brother Ernsti struggled along in medical school, the stewardship of the garden fell to you. Restless to immigrate to the US, you never really admitted that part of your motivation was to save the garden, and so you did, for decades quietly sending money every month to your parents, so they could keep the property. During their retirement your parents enjoyed the garden, year after year, planting vegetables and flowers in abundance. To be near their beloved plot of land they chose to live in an apartment just around the corner until Pappi died in 1972.

Meanwhile your brother, Ernsti, and his wife, Marianne, prospered, raised three children, and built a spacious, comfortable house, not on the street, but towards the front of the plot to keep most of the area free for flowers and vegetables. Your mother, now Oma to our children and Ur-Oma to our grandchildren, spent her latter years in a separate apartment, connected to, but not in the main house. For several decades, the eighties and the nineties, the Richters continued to putter around in the garden: Oma mostly in the front, mostly flowers; Ernsti, assisted by his family, mostly in the rear, vegetables and flowers.

With the new century came Ernsti's retirement from his pediatric x-ray practice in the local hospital and his full-time dedication to the garden . . . and how he loves it.

Engaged in the present this week, having buried Oma and now soaking up the glorious and rare summer sunshine, there is little thought of the future. When Ernsti and Marianne and I turn our toes up, who will be the next steward? Is there one or several? I don't think so. Our offspring are far away in the US. Ernsti's daughter, Anna, has her own family, house and garden in Kalten Kirchen, some 20-30 kilometers away. The "boys," Peter and Jonas, might not be able for such a momentous task.

Hamburg, Germany, 1943.
Just a few days after the bombing, the streets are swept,
the rubble is piled neatly and people are biking to work or
wherever. Life goes on. Here is proof positive that the human
spirit can and will survive. We can hope that the garden behind
these ruins will also somehow survive.

But for the moment, I choose to stay immersed in the present. I love looking out Oma's back window watching Ernsti watering his beloved roses. One day hungry developers, already lurking around, will buy the land, and bulldozers will tear everything down. Office buildings or condominiums will spring up like the dandelions Ernsti plucks daily from the lawn. Meanwhile I rejoice in your stewardship during the hard time and in Ernsti's stewardship here and now. Your unselfish foresight and generosity in the 50's, 60's, 70's, 80's, enriches the lives of all Richters on both sides of the ocean. Ernsti carries on the tradition through the '90's and now well into the new century.

FHCDS in the '50's

I wrote this piece in response to a questionnaire that came over the Internet from some current students at Far Hills Country Day School. I enjoyed reminiscing, and I hope I answered their questions and, of course, I added a few observations of my own. One difference between then and now is that our classes were small: seven of us in sixth grade; four of us in seventh; three of us in eighth. We got lots of individual attention, but if we were not well prepared for class, there was no place to hide!

The big sporting event for FHCDS students in the '50's was the World Series, particularly the rivalry between the Brooklyn Dodgers and the New York Giants in the playoffs. I was a Dodgers fan. During the playoffs and the World Series our Headmaster, Mr. Lambert F. Whetstone, listened to the game on the radio, and after every inning he tiptoed into each classroom and wrote the score on the board. We tried to contain our delight or dismay, but it was very hard.

Mr. Whetstone also taught history besides being Headmaster. He was very distinguished looking and real smart. Everyone respected him. He was also kind, rather like a grandfather. Before FHCDS he taught at one of those tony New England prep schools. I forget which one.

Another important and smart teacher was Mrs. Noling who taught English and everything else. She knew a couple of foreign languages too; I think French and Spanish—unusual in those days. She knew absolutely everything about English and American literature and shared her love for the classics with us. I read *The Yearling* with her in the sixth grade and was aghast that they killed the little deer. She wisely pointed out it had to happen or everyone would starve, a concept totally foreign to us well-fed students.

Madame Wadlow taught French and Art. She was another favorite and memorable teacher. She taught us all about France, not just the language.

She always spoke French to us, even in art class where she flew the French flag: "bleu, blanc, rouge."

Another memorable teacher was Mr. Rawlins who taught Latin. He was very nice but had terrible bad breath. When he leaned over my desk, I pulled back as far as I could. I think in retrospect he probably ate a lot of garlic. He had a nervous habit of jamming his hands into his pocket. One day he left his jacket hanging on his chair and we sewed up the pockets. Many titters that afternoon, we were never the suspects . . . luckily. A select group of us seventh and eights graders gathered the ingredients necessary for the crime: needles, thread and a growing boldness as days passed before he left his coat for us to fix. When he did leave it, the news spread like wildfire and soon the dastardly deed was done. Convulsed with laughter the rest of the day, we watched him try to jam his hands into his pockets. Good man that he was, he never said a word though surely he understood who had done him in. The next day his pockets were back to normal and so was our day, except for a lingering fear we might be busted, but that never happened. After that we always kind of respected him for clearly, "he could take a joke."

The building itself was a big dilapidated Victorian house, shielded from the busy road by a tall fence, what Westerners now call a "coyote fence," solid wood strips that kept the noise out and the children in. The main entrance to school was on the side away from the road. To the left was the secretary's office, where several busy women kept things going. To the right was a sort-of lobby/reception room beyond which was the Headmaster's office. Straight ahead—facing the road was the kindergarten whose noise drowned out any noise from the road that seeped through.

Upstairs to the right were the lower school classrooms which I don't remember, having arrived at FHCDS when I was a sixth grader. The Upper School was upstairs to the left. Mrs. Noling had her own room with her book-laden desk facing a horseshoe shaped table and plenty of chairs. (Plenty for our class of six or less!) My classroom was small—only six desks at most. I sat in the back row with my back to the window that looked on to the entrance and the parking lot. Downstairs to the left was the Art Room, everything in French because Madame Wadlow was proudly French. Downstairs in the basement we had "clay" where we made all kinds of creative pieces for Mrs. Snyder to glaze for us. Sadly, my best creation was accidentally broken by a second grader who grew up to be Steve Forbes. Our other famous graduate was Christy Todd Whitman. Even when she was in second grade, everyone knew who Christy Todd was.

Our school "bus" was a big, black limousine with three rows of seats that held my sister and me, the two Hofmanns, plus four McCashins, two Lovejoys, Diane Moyer, and Jos Wiley. Mr. Lupton, the math teacher, used to drive it. Now and then we would tease him and ask if he did funerals in his spare time. If he was in a good mood, we'd get a made-up gory story; if not, just a sharp "No!" He picked us Hofmanns up first and Jos, last so the ride to school, only fifteen minutes away, took at least a half an hour.

The playing fields were out beyond the parking lot as was the gymnasium which was off to the right. The school was divided into two teams, green and white, a tradition that I imagine still exists. I was a green. Competition in soccer, basketball, and softball was fierce. Besides for sports; the gym was used for assembly and school plays. At the far end was a stage, where Mrs. Noling directed a Gilbert and Sullivan play each year. Everyone in the school participated in some way. My favorite play was *The Yeomen of the Guard*.

Politically the big news was General Eisenhower running for President. I remember at the Far Hills Hunt Races, a cold blustery late October day just before the election, volunteers were handing out I LIKE IKE buttons and banners like crazy. My sister Carol, three years younger, (nine years to my twelve) and I proudly wore those buttons for weeks afterwards. Our father, a Rock Rib Republican liked IKE, and so did we. Well, after all, he did win World War II, so surely he could protect our country and us from all harm. There was never any doubt in our minds about that. We were totally safe.

The big technology breakthrough in the '50's was, of course, television. My parents bought a TV set (black and white, with a lot of "snow") for our grandfather who lived over the garage alone. He was old and couldn't get out much, so the idea was that the TV could keep him company (and, as I see it now, keep him engaged.) During the day for hours he would watch the McCarthy hearings where everyone was accused of being a Communist. Sometimes in the evening, Daddy Joe, as we called him, invited us over to watch George Burns and Gracie Allen, or "I Love Lucy." That was a real treat.

In 1952 the Olympics were held in Helsinki, Finland. We found the city on the map, and our mother went there to watch our neighbor, Arthur McCashin, compete. It was HUGE. Mr. McCashin, who lived on a farm just down the road, was the captain of our brand-new fledgling US Equestrian Team, formed after the cavalry was disbanded. There were no more military government-supported teams. Horses and riders trained at

McCashin's. They were our heroes (no heroines—women were not allowed to compete in the Equestrian Olympics in those days). Carol Durand, from out west, St. Louis, Missouri, to be exact, loaned her mount, Miss Budweiser, owned, by August Busch, owner of Budweiser beer, to Arthur and off he went to the Olympics, placing 5th individually, and leading our American team to the Bronze medal. It was HUGE.

The big bands on the radio in those days were Glenn Miller and Benny Goodman. Once we saw Benny Goodman live at the Waldorf Astoria Hotel in New York City. HUGE. Also famous, for us anyway, was Lester Lanin who often played at our little tea dances at the Essex Hunt Club.

Even though a year later when I was in high school, there were air raid drills, and we hid in the basement, at FHCDS there was no panic in our little pre-teen world. Mrs. Noling often quoted Robert Browning's poem:

> The year's at the spring, the day's at the morn,
> Morning's at seven, the hillside's dew-pearled,
> The lark's on the wing, the snail's on the thorn,
> God's in his heaven,
> All's right with the world."

Financial crises, and all world wide problems and wars escaped our notice. We lived on a farm and kept our Victory Garden long after World War II was over. There was no "yearling" to tear up our garden. Anyway, it was fenced. Besides we had President Eisenhower to protect us, so we felt totally safe, in spite of real and alleged Communists lurking out there and on TV.

Dogs I Have Slept With

I am a one-man dog, and now that man is gone, I sleep with dogs—dirt, fleas, dog hair, ticks and all. The saying that "if you sleep with dogs, you're gonna get fleas" is probably true, but so far I have been lucky. Max, my husband, my one man, did not like the dogs to sleep on the bed, so they respectfully slept on the floor, his on his side of the bed, mine on mine. However, whenever he was away, they hopped into bed with me, and I welcomed their company.

Long before I met Max I slept with dogs. The first was a Dalmatian, Rock Candy. She came with that name; I don't know its significance. She was a pretty dog who pursed her lips and growled when she was displeased. My tossing and turning in bed as a child was highly annoying to her, so I soon learned to lie still rather than make her cross. As it turned out I'm glad I mastered that skill early on. "Letting sleeping dogs lie" is a good skill to acquire going through life.

When Candy turned her toes up, our family acquired Bimbo, a gift from a friend, also a Dalmatian, and we named him aptly, as it turned out. He was high-strung and dumb, but cheerful and good-hearted. He latched on to me and never figured out that his lying crossways in my little, single bed simply did not work. Every night I had to kick him rudely until he rearranged himself lengthwise. Even so the bed was crowded, for he liked to lean against me. No matter how hard I shoved and kicked him, he quietly acquiesced and moved over. Candy would have growled fiercely and possibly even bitten me.

After Max and I married and moved from Manhattan to the country, we found a dog in the *New York Times*, a German shorthaired pointer like the ones Max's family had when he was growing up. We gave him a good German name, Fritz. Fritz was no dummy; he figured out the rules straight away. When Max was home, he slept in his basket at the foot of our bed.

When Max was away, he slept in bed lengthwise with me. The command, "Into your *Korbchen*" would send him high tailing it to his basket from anywhere in the house.

I have found over the years that a good barometer of a dog's intelligence and temperament is how quickly he figures out the house and particularly the bed rules. Several other issues have some bearing on the question. The Corgis, Bear who brightened our lives in the '80's and Dylan in the '90's, were both too long-bodied and short-legged to get on the bed. They slept cheerfully on the floor next to the bed for their entire lives.

Bullet, our second German shorthaired pointer was smart enough and obliging; besides he understood and abided by the rules. He soon figured out that sleeping crossways on the bed was not an option.

With the arrival of our first Jack Russell, Duke, son Hans's dog, all rules were challenged. Duke slept with Hans, end of story, that story anyway. Duke rejected and revised once and for all Max's rule, no dogs on the furniture. (After all, in the Germany of his childhood, dogs were not even allowed in the house!) Smacks and scolding were of no avail, and finally we just had to give in. Soon all the dogs even the Golden Retrievers were luxuriating all over the furniture. The Goldens, first Clay in the '70's and '80's and Sam-I-Am in the '90's and beyond, respectfully stay off the bed regardless of whether Max is around or not, but they like to luxuriate on the couch.

My experience with Jack Russells so far has been that they have very little respect for any rules at all, the exception being our two Irish Jack Russells, first Sarah and now her sister, Sister. A very strict upbringing in Ireland apparently set them on the right track; neither ever tested Max's bed rule. On the other hand, the "apple of my eye," in fact, the orchard of my eye for eighteen years, Pinocchio was not above testing the bed rule. Occasionally when we were fast asleep, he would hop up on the lower corner of my side of the bed. As soon as one of us stirred, he was down, back in his own bed.

The Jack Russell's bed next to my side of the bed has not seen a live body in it since Max left us, but Sam, Max's dear, old Golden Retriever, slept faithfully on the floor on Max's side of the bed. He was still respectful of his master's wishes, or perhaps he was just too old and stiff to hop up on the bed. I preferred to believe the former as he was still able to struggle up the stairs every evening and even snored on the couches sometimes. His snoring forced me to sleep on Max's side of the bed, so I could reach down and pet him to quiet the noise. Every morning he jammed his head between the desk and the bed and smiled at me as I stroked his dear, grey nose before we started the day.

The two Jack Russells—mother, Sister, and daughter, Miracle—are proprietary about the bed. They wouldn't even permit, Blitz, the German shorthaired pointer, who was twice their combined size, as is his successor, Rouxpert, to enter the room, let alone jump on the bed. Like Bimbo the Dalmatian of my childhood, they're too dumb and agreeable to argue. Rouxpert also sleeps outside the open bedroom door or downstairs on a couch. Sister usually retires to the bed right after her dinner, partly to keep the others out and partly to prevent being shut out herself. One ironclad rule about dogs and my bed is that dogs who go swamping and are caked with mud eat their dinners outside and sleep in the barn. There ARE limits.

Lonesome for our dear, departed Sam, I visited some adorable Golden Retriever puppies, but a puppy was not really what I wanted, so I turned to the Internet: GoldenRetrieverRescue.com. A blizzard of emails clogged my computer; foreclosures and the ensuing smaller rental apartments rendered many fine dogs homeless.

Trumbo, an aged, deaf, lame fellow caught my eye. He had been picked up, starving and nameless, on a country road near Albany, treated for Lyme Disease and neutered by Peppertree Rescue. He was placed in a foster home, unwanted for months until I came along. He was exactly what I wanted.

After filling out numerous forms to prove I was a worthy dog owner, I collected Trumbo up in Albany, heaved him awkwardly into the car and brought him home. Low maintenance, he mostly ignores the other dogs, sleeps a lot, and roams around the fenced in backyard. The open kitchen door enables him to go in and out at will. He doesn't do stairs anymore, so he is the downstairs dog and a kind, pleasant friend to me.

A relatively new member of the family is Popcorn, son of Miracle who several years ago produced a litter of eight puppies: four black-and-tans like their father, my sister's Scout About, three black-and-whites, and one brown-and-white for me. Popcorn is simply a typical Jack Russell: erect tail and arrogant attitude. His grandmother, Sister, and his mother, Miracle, keep him from getting too out of line.

Blitz and Sam are gone now, Blitz in a tragic accident while Sam succumbed to old age. Blitz's brother, in fact, his littermate, Rouxpert, has come to live with me for two years while his family is in Angola, where dogs are not welcome. Rouxpert is heartbreakingly like Blitz, so he is a welcome, if temporary, member of the family.

If you make a habit of sleeping with dogs, you will get more sleep if you "let sleeping dogs lie" whenever possible. Lying still also sometimes works if your dogs are early risers. My Jack Russells start twirling at about 5 am every day. If I don't have something important that has to get done, I can "play possum" and fool them for an hour or so. A tiny bonus is that if you lie still, you are more apt to fall asleep again. Except for some snoring, they seldom disturb me at night. The flip side of that is they would probably sleep through robberies and fires, so I lock the doors at night and keep the smoke alarms up to speed. Despite their occasional itching, scratching, and snoring, they are snugglers, and for the most part, good company. Like her father, Pinocchio, Miracle sleeps behind my knees; Sister, facing me, so she knows exactly whether we are really getting up or not. What's best about sleeping with dogs is their exuberant enthusiasm when it is time to get up. Their eager twirling and smiling gets the day off to a good start.

Epilogue: My friend Nick tells two slightly shaggy dog tales. The first is about a dinner guest who arrived dressed in black velvet. His Jack Russell took a shine to her and spent the evening in her lap covering the black velvet with his plentiful white hairs.

The next day when she took the dress to the cleaners, the gal at the counter asked, "who you sleep wid last night?"

"Oh, it was just a dog."

"Ain't de all?" was her reply.

Nick's second story was about a friend who was grousing that he caught his wife in bed with his best friend . . .

"Who?" Nick asked incredulously.

"Rover," was the answer.

And so our dogs brighten our lives, even when we just talk about them.

My Two Favorite Fleabags

If you sleep with dogs, you're gonna' get fleas.
If you travel with dogs, you'll sleep in flea bags.

On the road from horse show to horse show I sample many fleabags over the year, and a favorite fleabag motel that permits dogs, is the Southampton Village Motel on Long Island, when we horse show every week before Labor Day. I discovered it about twenty years ago because it was cheap and cheerful, AND it allows dogs to stay there too. It's not cheap anymore, but dogs are still welcome, so here we are again.

When we first stayed there, it was definitely seedy, a row of ten rooms where paint was peeling, inside and out. Beside and behind the rooms is a lovely garden, grassy and edged with voluminous flowers, bushes, hydrangeas and such, and finally enclosed by a tall stockade fence. The garden with its unpretentious furniture, several tables and chairs, is pretty much the same, but everything else has been fluffed up.

The rooms are small, so small that one person has to stay in bed while the other dresses (my only roommate recently is a dog, sometimes two, who obligingly lie on the bed). Likewise, the bathroom is small but big enough to turn around in. Major upgrades in the bathroom are significant. The flimsy, worn towels have been replaced by voluminous, thick, large, terrycloth. Now there is a little basket of Gilchrist and Soames soap, shampoo, conditioner, body lotion, and even a shower cap. The Kleenex box is enclosed in wicker. Best of all is the water pressure; the shower is like a fire hose instead of water dribbling out of the faucet.

My freshly-painted room features several framed posters from previous years of the horse show, possibly slapped up on the walls during horse show week to help us horsy types feel at home. WiFi is available, and the TV screen is big and offers cable, free of charge. Best of all, the swaybacked hammock bed has been replaced by a firm, comfortable mattress. The fluffy duvet and big, square, European pillows are much better than threadbare blankets and the old, tired, flat pillows. A large bottle of Perrier and real glass glasses are on the nightstand along with a printed welcome note. Other amenities are an air conditioner and a refrigerator for beer and cheese for when I'm too tired to go out. The young, energetic owners are eager to please, and there is nothing not to like about this charming little place. It is clean and there are no fleas here. It is no wonder it is a favorite fleabag motel, admittedly expensive over Labor Day weekend . . . .

The other favorite fleabag is a spacious cabin at Schulti's Motor Lodge in Lake Placid where we show for two weeks early in the summer. The cabin has fewer amenities; the beds are swaybacked; the towels, worn; the bathmat, paper; the water flow, torrential, a plus. There is no air conditioning, (seldom needed in Lake Placid), curtains are frayed, but it's roomy and comfortable. The full kitchen, complete with table and chairs, is perfect for eating in with family or friends and for catching up on book work and writing. The TV has two channels, one provides news from the outside world and the other runs videos from the horse show 24/7, always good entertainment. Outside is a swimming pool, usually noisy and full of kids and chlorine. The dogs have plenty of room to run and play, though a busy road nearby necessitates my being watchful.

Mrs. Schulti and her husband are both German, so the place is immaculate. We have fun jabbering in German, and, of course in the old days Max got along famously with them even though they are from the south of Germany and he was from Hamburg in the north. (Inside the country the Germans are very chauvinistic about their own regions but when abroad they are best friends. A shared language, despite the dialects, makes for fine bonding). Early in the morning down in the basement Mr. Schulti, who is a highly-regarded photographer, serves coffee, strong enough to trot a horse across, but it's nice to fill our mugs on our way to the horse show, and by the time we get there we are wide awake and ready to start the day. He also makes lots of ice so we can load our coolers to chill our drinks and to fill the ice boots for our old horses who need special care after jumping high.

Another nice feature of Schulti's is that it is still cheap—$50-$60 per night depending on the size of the cabin. My traditional cabin Maple is big and cost $60 a night, but worth every penny. Other fleabags, mostly Motel 6's scattered around the country, are fine, plenty good enough, but generic. In the towns of Southampton and Lake Placid, even the fleabags have their own charm. Every year we leave a deposit to reserve rooms for the next year in hope that, God willing, we will be back.

Our Neighbor's Woods and Fields

For over thirty years we have enjoyed riding our horses through our neighbor's woods. The tall, pine trees adjoining our fields stretch toward the sky and nearby the beech and maple forest extents forever in all directions. It is what Vermonters call "a clean woods," very little underbrush, so over the years we have made countless trails. Hence the one hundred acres of forest and farm feels like three or four hundred. Some vast tracts of land so close to New York City, a mere thirty five miles away, are surprising and delightful.

Shortly after we bought our farm over thirty years ago, our neighbor graciously invited us to tea. Even then he was an aged, stooped, white-whiskered gentleman, a rather upper-class Edwardian fellow. As we entered his home, a real mansion, not a McMansion, his wife was nowhere to be seen; deceased, but her tastes lived on; she insisted that their charming colonial home, dating from the mid-eighteenth century, be painted pink, a rather loud pink at that. It was her favorite color, and he honored it for as long as he lived.

The butler served tea in the library warmed by a cheerful fire. He poured the tea from an heirloom, silver teapot and handed around the steaming paper-thin porcelain cups. After tea we walked all around his estate admiring his collection of farm animals from the rooster who woke us up every day to his herd of steers who often escaped from his fields and came to visit us, knocking over tubs of grain and leaving cow plops in the barn aisle. There were also goats and sheep, well-behaved, stay-at-homes, and some brightly colored exotic birds. His pride and joy of the farm was the Mill House next to the lake at the waterfall. It was his "study," but what he studied, I'm not sure. His ancestors and indeed himself in his youth, were avid, big game hunters in Africa and later Alaska, so the walls were covered with the heads of countless dusty, moth-eaten lions, tigers, elephants, rhinos, and, last but not least, a moose.

He was proud of his appointment as Ambassador to England under Eisenhower, rather a plum, to say the least, and he admitted that maintaining a one-hundred-acre farm in Bedford, New York was an expensive undertaking, particularly because he "had" to keep his cherished Park Avenue address in the City. He had sold off several lots along the road to keep the cash flow "up to speed," (presumably to support himself in the style to which he had become accustomed: mansion, maids and butler.) His children were grown, and he lived quite happily alone, well cared for by his staff. Over the years we exchanged Christmas cards and occasional pleasantries at the post office. Well into his nineties, he moved on, and his son is likewise determined to hang on to the farm. A paunchy, prosperous-looking baby boomer, he wisely sold his father's New York apartment as well as forty acres of the woods adjoining our farm to a famous, young actor and his wife who fell in love with the beautiful woods and fields. Of course, our neighbor gave them a right of way, so they proceeded to install a mile-long, paved driveway from the road to the top of the hill where presumably one day they would build a McMansion. Trying not to be disgruntled neighbors, we looked on the bright side: better one McMansion than ten four-acre lots which is what a developer would have done. Rumors of an impending divorce and a tanking economy make us hopeful that the status quo will continue for a while.

The son rented out the big house and spends his weekends at the Mill House overlooking the lake. A few steers have been confined to the lower fields near the old dilapidated barns. Except for the new owner's paved driveway to the "back forty," the remaining fields and woods are virtually abandoned, and we are welcome to ride out there anytime.

The recent weeks of glorious fall weather inspired me to clear old trails and cut some new ones where our neighbor used to pasture his cattle. After the old man turned his toes up, his steers were securely fenced in close to the barns. His children intend to hang on to the farm, all one-hundred-acres of it, and because we are welcome to ride over there, I spent the last three days cutting barbed wire fencing and clearing brush; now there is a lovely network of trails.

As I worked away, I was reminded of my Vermont friend, Denny Emerson, who wrote a lovely piece about clearing brush:

> Today I was cutting up on our hill, in a section of land that doesn't look out over any modern "improvements," no road, no phone or electric lines, no houses—just huge, old maples and hilly pastureland. It was cloudy, with intermittent showers, and there was one moment when the only sounds I could hear were the soft pattering of falling leaves, no cars, no chainsaws, no airplanes, nothing out of nature. In the foreground a herd of Holsteins meandered by grazing.
>
> I suddenly thought that this could just as easily have been 1850, or 1905, or 1920. It was something really quite precious, and fading rapidly, I suspect, a moment of "old Vermont," that we can remember from 40 or 50 years ago.

Likewise I was far from civilization and admittedly sometimes a little bit lost. It's heartening to find out once again that wilderness still exists so close to the City. Because I worked out there on weekends, there was little noise from the outside world except for an occasional car swishing by on the road nearly a mile away. Birds chirped merrily and crows cawed angrily as I toiled away. Squirrels bustled around anxiously watching that I did not uncover and discover their winter stash of nuts. Two separate herds of deer browsed unconcernedly nearby. While an older group of seven or eight doe was guarded by a big, strong buck that crossly shook his six or seven-point rack of antlers at me, a younger, smaller group accompanied by a young buck sporting a two or three-point rack meandered around as well. I hope they will all escape the hunters' sharp arrows next month.

The property has been in the family for generations. Most of the land wooded and open has been fenced forever, first by stone walls, now rather tumble down, then by split rail fencing, now rotted and broken, and finally by barbed wire. Land-poor farm owners like us just patch, patch, patch. No fancy fencing for them or us. My piss-ant wire cutters were no match for that wire, even though it was old and rusty. Much had been replaced with even tougher wire, featuring sharper barbs. On the second day of my trail-blazing project I came armed with real cutters and easily cut a few gaps between the various lush, green fields where we look forward to cantering around this wonderful tract of land for years to come.

Robert Frost asserted and actually was questioning in "Mending Wall" that "Good fences make good neighbors." In the twenty-first century we are trying to tear down walls, starting with the Berlin Wall, and put out of work his "old stone savages" that build them. The jury is still out whether tearing down walls is a good idea. I would like to think that it is. In any case, there will be no miles of upscale, high-end white, board fencing on the property anytime soon.

The children, current owners, are too frugal to squander their money on glitz. They would rather own one-hundred-acres wild, overgrown land than fifty acres of manicured lawns, boxwood hedges, fancy fencing, and barns. This is old money at its finest: down to earth and unpretentious. The love for open land is quintessentially American; it no longer stretches "from sea to shining sea," but we try to preserve it as best we can, even thirty-five miles from Times Square.

Block Island

The best story in our family about Block Island is the first one which my husband Max delighted in telling over and over, especially in his later years. To secure his pilot's license he had to fly solo to a destination within one hour of Westchester Airport where he received his flight training. On his map he drew a circle using the airport as its midpoint having computed how fast he would be flying and hence how far he could go. On land and in the air Max was always a map man.

Fitting neatly just inside the perimeter of his circle and outfitted with a suitable airport was Block Island, Rhode Island, just across from Montauk at the end of Long Island. Always the explorer, Max eagerly chose the then-unknown island as his destination and off he flew. Before landing he circled several times admiring the infinite sandy beaches, the tall, clay cliffs, the weathered, grey houses, and the open, moor-like pastures, crisscrossed by stone walls. At dinner that night he was so excited about his discovery, the wonderful island he found, he did not say much at all about the excitement, the bird-like freedom of flying, but certainly the flying alone for the first time must have been thrilling.

Having landed smoothly, he taxied over to the shabby, little grey building, parked his plane and walked around to the front, wondering what to do next as the gentle, salt wind tousled his hair. Just then a battered, old Chevy with huge tail fins pulled up. A sign on the roof declared it was "Maizie's Cab." The driver, a large grey-haired woman, Maizie Lewis herself, leaned out the window and shouted,

"Young man, get in. I'll show you the island," and so she did, all seven-by-three miles of it, as she gave a running commentary on the island's history and present state.

Max was enchanted, for Block Island reminded him very much of Herligenhafen, a little fishing village/summer holiday town where his family vacationed for years before the war and to which they fled during the war to escape the major bombing of their home town, Hamburg. When he could finally get a word in edgewise, he asked, "Is it possible to rent a little place here? I'd like to bring my family on holiday."

"Well," Maizie snorted, we have the best on the whole island right on our farm" and drove him straightaway to Lewis Farm, which had been in the family since 1812. Too old to farm, the resourceful Lewis family converted the various barns, large and small, even the chicken coop, into summer vacation homes and cottages. The charming, grey, shingled buildings were cozy and rustic inside. "Just right," thought Max and signed up for two weeks the next summer, and we've been going there ever since.

For almost forty years, our family of four—husband Max, two sons, Hans and Philip and me—have rented a place on Lewis Farm for the last two weeks of July. First we were in Maizie's nephew's home, Plover Hill on the point, which offers the best view of the Atlantic Ocean on the entire East Coast. The next year the nephew decided not to rent, so we moved into "The Building" a one-bedroom cottage overlooking acres of pasture where cattle graze and beyond the fields crisscrossed by stone walls, the sea. Luckily the boys were old enough to pitch a tent and live outside, for accommodations were tight. The next year the Small Barn with its three bedrooms was available. Eventually we graduated to the spacious Big Barn with its cathedral ceiling and upstairs loft. It felt very large but at the same time cozy, for in one corner couches were grouped, so all could see the wide pastures and the vast ocean. The sunsets into the ocean were glorious indeed. In recent years we've downsized from the family of four to two, Philip and me, (Hans and his family having moved to California), from two weeks to one, from the Big Barn back to the Building, and we love every moment we are there.

This year in front of the airport we installed a wooden bench in Max's honor, so pilots and passengers alike could at least sit down as they figured out where they were going next.

Peri Wahn: Then and Now

Our farm in Vermont has been in the family for well over sixty years. In 1946 when my sister Carol and I were youngsters, our parents bought the place—house, barn and one hundred acres—for $2,500, partly to escape the ravages of the polio epidemic in New Jersey. In our hearts it has always been a safe refuge from whatever was menacing in the outside world.

The farm, abandoned for a decade, was discovered by our neighbors across the valley. Old horsy friends from the days my parents lived in Boston, they spent summers at their Vermont farm with the children, dogs, and horses. They persuaded my parents it was a good life, a fine way to raise kids, and they knew of "just the place" for us to buy. Their daughters, June and Debbie, several years older than my sister Carol and me, were soon to become our idols and mentors.

June and Debbie rode their horses all over the countryside, and of the many abandoned farms nearby, they loved our little house on the hill the best. At the end of a long, uphill road on the top of a mountain it felt like the top of the world, looking out at mountains receding in the distance.

The girls named the farm "Peri Wahn," which means Journey's End in Persian. One of them was engrossed in a summer-reading-assigned book, the name of which they cold not remember later, so it is lost forever. What we all got out of that book was the name for the farm, Peri Wahn, and it is indeed that, sitting up there at the end of the road on the top of the mountain. Both girls' ashes are scattered there as are my mother's and several other close friends and animals from over the years.

Our first journey to Peri Wahn in 1947 was long and arduous, to say the least. We left home in New Jersey at 6 am sharp to be ahead of the traffic. In those days, there were no four-lane highways anywhere. (Eisenhower, not yet President, had not started to implement his boyhood plan to connect this vast nation with an Interstate highway program.)

We took Route 22 East to Manhattan, over the Pulaski Skyway, and the George Washington Bridge and then on forever north to Rutland, Vermont and Route 4 to Woodstock. Driving east recently in the dark on Route 4 over sixty years later, I felt like it was still an endless road. From Woodstock north the roads in those days were not paved: bumpy, winding and dark.

Our little, crowded Jeep groaned as it pulled the heavy, homemade two-horse trailer up the long, welcoming hills. The rig was loaded to the hilt: a horse and our pony in the trailer, four people and three dogs in the Jeep and all our belongings. My mother drove, my grandmother, her mother, road shotgun, my sister and I sat across from each other on the metal seats in the back, the three dogs at our feet. We were barely out of the driveway in New Jersey when we started asking "Are we there yet?" Finally, over twelve hours later, we were "there."

Luckily our friends across the valley had extra stalls, extra beds, and a delicious dinner waiting for us. I only vaguely remember unloading the horses, eating supper, and falling into bed. All I remember is that it was great to be "there," whatever that was.

At dawn a crystal clear, glorious Vermont summer day welcomed us, and across the valley we could see our little house high on the mountain. Getting there was not so easy. June and Debbie rode the horse and pony over, for we knew the Jeep would never be able to pull them up the narrow, steep, winding road. While Mother and Nana unpacked, they showed us all around our house and barn, which they knew so well. The place was "furnished," somewhat; it was retro-'20's furniture, old, but not "antique," declared my mother. The kitchen table still sits where it was when we walked into the house. Surrounded by the same chairs, it sports a "new," now forty-year-old linoleum top and the chairs have cushions.

Of great interest to the four of us that day was an old, cowhide trunk we found in the back of a closet upstairs. Because it was lined with newspaper from South Carolina in the late 1850's my grandmother, who grew up in Kentucky, surmised it was a slave trunk, carried this far by some poor Negro seeking freedom. Built in the early eighteenth century, the house was reputedly a stop on the Underground Railway, and probably it was.

Unable to afford installing both running water and electricity, my parents had opted to get water first, definitely a good plan. The water came from a spring on the hillside behind us, and Archie Charon, a French Canadian contractor my father befriended, assured us that gravity would bring the water down to us, and it did.

My grandmother knew all about cooking on wood stoves and lighting kerosene lamps. How lucky we were that she lived with us and could guide us through those early days. She loved the big, black, wood stove in the kitchen where she fried bacon and eggs and taught us about Farmer's Toast, slathered with butter and done in the oven. In the afternoons she often baked delicious cakes. Lemon was my favorite.

Having no electricity meant we had no refrigerator. There was an icebox in the hall that worked, but, of course, there had to be ice. Twice a week we journeyed to Woodstock, the nearest town, ten miles away, for ice and supplies. First were errands (hardware store, pharmacy, etc.) then groceries, and finally the ice house. The proprietor, old Mr. Leonard, ushered us cordially into his cold, dark, sawdust-strewn ice house to pick out the size ice block we needed. "Not too big; it won't fit. Not too small; it will melt too soon," he cautioned us merrily. Last winter's harvest of deer hung from the ceiling, a dozen heads down, back legs tied to the rafters. We learned first hand the expression, "It's cold enough to hang meat here." It was, and he hung his own deer and his friends'. Ice block selected and paid for, it was stuffed into the back of the Jeep by Mr. Leonard himself, and we headed home. It was so heavy all hands had to help get it from the Jeep to the icebox, but we always managed.

A good incentive to stay quiet in our warm beds in the morning was the rule that the first person up had the job to empty the pail of melted ice water under the icebox, not an easy task for a small child, so we made a habit of laying low until we heard someone else stirring.

Speaking of beds, they were horrific, like hammocks. The previous owners left them when they moved out ten years before, so they were musty and dusty as well: okay for the mice but not us. Sister Carol and I were delighted with the bunk bed replacements. Friends from back home could come visit; there were plenty of beds. Fifty years later after our parents turned their toes up, and I inherited the farm, the first thing I did was replace those beds, now themselves like hammocks. In tossing out those old, tired beds, I was putting to bed, so to speak, our old selves, our family, and friends, many now gone themselves. Dozens, maybe even hundreds of people have slept in those beds. Luckily, the beds can't talk; "what happens in Vermont stays in Vermont," as the saying goes. Out with the bunk beds went my sister Carol's and my own childhood and friends as well as my sons' childhood and friends. And now we have the new bunk beds with their twenty-first century sidebars which my granddaughters and their friends enjoy in total safety. Carol and I always slept on the upper bunks

Peri Wahn: Then and Now.
The Hofmann Family at Peri Wahn in 1947:
Nana Kain, Sister Carol, Father—"Big Phil,"
the Author, Mother Mary and assorted dogs.
It looks like Appalachia, but we loved our frontier life.

Peri Wahn in 1950 is still the same today.

Breakfast at Peri Wahn, August 2003.
The 3 M's—My husband, Max, and two granddaughters,
Maxine and Margot enjoy a fifty-year-old tradition.

and fell out of bed now and then. I know first hand how much it hurts to land on the floor from that height.

The other beds saw plenty of action when the house was in its "love-nest" phase, during my college years and after. Max, first lover and then husband, and I spent many happy weekends here. When the children came along, the farm resumed its role as our vacation home and often, always over New Years, every bed in the house was full. The first thing I did was replace those beds, now themselves also like hammocks. Now we have lovely, new state-of-the-art beds, and our warm bodies find comfort in them.

Still today, over sixty years later, Peri Wahn lies in our hearts as a safe refuge whenever the outside world threatens. The weekend after 9/11 our sons, now grown, sent Max and me to Vermont, the car loaded with bottled water, beer, and imperishable provisions which we dutifully stored in the basement. Realists would point out that if there were a national disaster, getting to Vermont from wherever we were would be more arduous than our first journey, if not impossible altogether. Boston, a likely terrorist target, is only a few hours away, and anyway weapons of mass destruction will get to you no matter where you are. Well, we stocked the house and comforted ourselves that we would lie low there until the danger was past.

An Evocative Object: My Saddle

Someone was telling me recently about a book or article she read describing evocative objects: things in our lives, in our homes and barns that summon and call forth memories and, though considered by many obsolete, still are in use. Being a real hoarder, I have lots of such items lying around, and many I continue to use. The most precious is my saddle, a gift from my first, last, and only billionaire client. People who do not ride have no idea how important one's saddle is. Most riders are fanatics about their saddles, and so am I, even today. Some refuse to ride in any other saddle but their own. I am not that fussy. There are admittedly other good saddles out there—*Butets, Devacoux, Antares*—to name a few, besides the old standbys—the Italian *Parianis*, the German Stubbens—both of which I rode on many years ago BMH, Before My *Hermès*, still a highly-regarded saddle, and always costly, $2000 in the '70's (two-thirds of my yearly salary then. I was teaching high school English!), well over $5000 now.

Known in the barn as "the Judy Richter" because of the worn, tarnished brass nameplate on the back, it is a "*Hermès*, Bill Steinkraus model, dahling." Acquired in the mid '70's when Billy headed our Olympic Team and was a recent winner of the Gold Medal (in 1968), the saddle is flat, and has little stuffing, unlike the sofas of today. Billy wanted to be close to his horse, and so do I.

Back in the '70's my client called me from Paris.

"I'm here at *Hermès*," and "What size, um," (I thought she was going to say gloves) . . . "saddle do you use? I want to get one for you."

First I was speechless, they cost thousands, and then I stuttered, "seventeen inch," the measurement from pommel (front) to cantle (back). In those days *Hermès* was the Cadillac of saddles, and, to my way of thinking, it still is.

She brought it home on the plane, and I still ride in it every day, thirty-five years later. New saddles are like new shoes; it takes a while to break them in, and each rider breaks his in differently, so we don't particularly like having other people ride in our saddles, whether they are new or old like mine. An evocative element of this saddle, any saddle, any horseback riding astride (not aside . . . sidesaddle, a favorite with Victorian ladies . . . or their men, in any case) is the erotic. Straddling a horse's back has orgasmic undertones, often felt but seldom mentioned as we concentrate on the work at hand: breaking the bucking colt, finding the next jump, winning the class at the horse show. Riding horses is a very here and now endeavor, and I find that so many good, bad, and indifferent creatures have carried that saddle that when I try to remember them, they gallop right out of my brain, as I throw it on the next horse I'm planning to ride.

Nowadays there are almost as many saddle experts as there are saddles, many of them intermediate riders who have no idea what they are talking about. On the other hand, there are veterinarians and chiropractors, riders and trainers who do indeed recognize a good saddle that fits the horse and rider well. There is a whole cottage industry of saddle makers who travel to the various barns to sell their wares, custom made saddles for horse and rider. Such a breezy salesman was in the other day to outfit some intermediate riders in a tenant's barn. They couldn't wait to spend thousands of dollars for his wonder saddle, made-to-order and ready in six months. Meanwhile what do they do? Ride bareback?

Does that mean that if I have six horses I need half a dozen saddles? "They," of course claim" yes." The experts consider my saddle obsolete which suits me fine. So am I. My one size seventeen inch fits nearly all horses, not the very high-withered and/or low-backed ones, but even they can tolerate my saddle if I use compensating saddle pads. Low-backed horses need "keyhole pads," pads shaped like a keyhole or a lollipop to prop up the back of the saddles. High-withered horses need a hole cut out of the front of the pad to make room for the withers. It's not that hard, and the proof of the pudding is that my horses' backs and withers are not sore. Besides saving money on these extravagantly expensive saddles, I don't have many vet and chiropractor bills. A win, win, win situation with the biggest win being that I am perfectly comfortable in this thirty-five-year-old relic of a saddle. Now the leather is thin and worn. The seat is cracked around the edges. The little leather loops that hold the stirrup strap ends secure are nearly worn through. Saddle makers have offered to replace the worn parts, but I don't want to change anything. Since I am closing in on the finish line, this saddle will last long enough for me.

Admittedly, if I were riding over huge jumps in international, world-class competition I would investigate the saddle market carefully, for at that level, every detail matters, but I am not at that level or even close, and my seventeen inch Bill Steinkraus *Hermès* still works for me as well as it did the first day I sat on it. Recently I took my client who bought me the saddle out to dinner to remind her that I still appreciate her generosity and her abiding friendship. My saddle was and is still one evocative object.

Sixty Years at the Devon Horse Show

Driving to the Devon Horse Show this year I realized that I have been coming to this prestigious event on the Main Line, outside of Philadelphia for over sixty years, a lifetime as it were. Nowhere in the world have the ups and downs of horse showing been more evident to me that at Devon.

Horse shows are like final exams. They give you a chance to test yourself and your horses, a test not just against the current competition, but a realistic barometer of where you are. At home many of us can cruise smoothly around a course, just like Joe Fargis and Touch of Class in the 1984 Olympics at Los Angeles where they won the Gold Medal. However, in a competitive situation not on home turf, it is harder to rise to the occasion. At Devon "where champions meet" it is easy to lose your focus when you see the best competitors from all over the country and hear the noisy crowd in the towering grandstands. Devon was and is, now and forever, a big deal. Situated on a giant city block, the show grounds are surrounded by the rows of stables that face toward the inside. Light blue and white are the traditional Devon colors, seen everywhere from the prize list that comes in the mail in March to the catalogue on sale at the show listing the exhibitors, to the committee stand overlooking the main ring, once the Wanamaker Oval, now the Dixon Oval. Inside the boundaries of the stables near the Dixon Oval and grandstands, is a second ring as big as the first and a large open area where riders exercise and train their horses. Extra barns across the road house the majority of the entries. Only the elite, Olympic medalists and long time supporters of the horse show, have stalls handy to the rings. We usually have stalls across the road; our competing for sixty years is not enough, but we don't care. The stalls are roomy and airy; the barn aisles, wide and spacious. It's nice back there, away from the hubbub of the horse show.

Our first venture to this august venue was in the early fifties. I was nine years old; my sister, Carol, six. Our father drove our 1948 Jeep, Mother rode shotgun, Carol and I sat on the iron benches behind, and in back of us was the pony and cart in the oak-floored, plywood-sided, home-made (by our father) trailer. Nowadays the grey pony "Misty Morn" would be called a "rescue pony;" she was on her way to Bunchie's, the monthly knacker sale in Metuchen, New Jersey, when our parents bought her for $150. Their friend from Boston, a horse dealer who bought horses out West and sold them for slaughter, always stayed at our farm the night before the auction, so we got to pick through the goods. Nearly all our horses in those days were "rescues," but we didn't think of them as that. We believed they were "diamonds in the rough," as our mother used to say. Potential champions? After all we *were* soon to be at the place "Where Champions Meet." It said so on the prize list and the sign over the ingate.

We left home at 5 am. It was still pitch dark, but the white pony was easy to see as we shoved her into the dark trailer next to the cart she was to pull later. Wisely leaving the three dogs behind, we crawled into the Jeep, already crammed with brushes and pails, the saddle and bridle, the driving harness, and, of course, our horse show clothes. In those days there was no Jersey Turnpike so it took hours, five at least, to get from the middle of New Jersey to Devon.

Finally we arrived about 10 am. My class, the walk-trot, was scheduled to be at 11. With no time to be awed by the biggest horse show we had ever seen, we set to work washing manure stains off Misty's rear end while Mother braided her mane. Then, while I dressed, they tacked her up, Mother picked up my number at the horse show office, and we dashed to the ring my pigtails flying, and got there just in time. The ring master, dressed in a top hat and red coat, sounded his horn for the class to start and then shouted instructions: WALK . . . TROT . . . WALK . . . REVERSE . . . WALK . . . TROT . . . WALK . . . LINE UP . . . . I remembered to check my diagonals at the trot and managed to stay out of trouble, not easy in a class of twenty or twenty-five ponies and riders, some of them very fancy-looking. I was called out third and proudly collected my yellow ribbon, quite chuffed, but not for long.

Next was the lead line, we shortened the stirrups a lot, tossed tiny sister Carol on, and my tall father led her around the awesome Wanamaker Oval, by then surrounded by crowds in the grandstands. Of course, Carol won; she always did, starting then, but there was no time to gloat. We had to hitch the pony to the cart and get back in the ring. I drove and Carol rode shotgun; we can't remember if we got a ribbon, but what a day it was! After touring the fair and riding the merry-go-round and the ferris wheel, we bought some famous Devon Fudge, loaded up and went home.

My next trip to Devon, several years, later, was stressful. By then I was jumping Pony Hunter Courses. With twenty-twenty hindsight I see that Misty, the rescue pony, was not a very good jumper. Besides she was green and inexperienced; so was I, but that did not deter us. Also I was to ride Itsy Bitsy, a very hot, antsy, grey pony that belonged to a friend who was afraid of her. I was too, but I was too proud to admit it.

Off we went to Devon, parents, calm and unconcerned; Carol, excited to ride in the walk-trot; and me, nervous. I opted to ride Misty first, and we staggered around the course, glad to canter through the finish markers. Next I had to ride Itsy who was chomping at the bit before I got on her. I gritted my teeth; she charged into the ring and tore around the course. Grateful to have survived, I pulled up, got off her, and never rode her again. Carol, of course, won her class; we did the fair, ate the fudge, and went home.

For the next few years our focus at Devon was on the Parent-and-Child class in which a parent and child rode tandem, one behind the other, over a course of jumps, and the Family Class, where the family rides abreast on the flat. One year Mother and I won the Parent-and-Child class on our two grey rescues, Twilight and Foggy Morn. Our joy was somewhat mitigated because our father's horse, Copper Morn, also a rescue, was a horrible jumper, so he and sister Carol did not get a ribbon. All was forgiven, however, when we won the family class with mismatched horses—two greys, a bay and a chestnut. Riding abreast at the walk, trot, and canter, we stuck together like glue, unlike some of the other entries that matched beautifully and were scattered all over the ring. It was huge, and we were all terribly proud, munching our fudge on the way home in our rattletrap horse van, having outgrown the two-horse trailer.

A few years later we did not fare so well in the Family Class though this time our horses were perfectly matched. Instead of our trusty old rescue sleds, three of us were mounted on hot Thoroughbred mares. They even got my father's solid Mr. George riled up, and after prancing raggedly around the ring, we retired before the class was over, and that ended for good our family class efforts. The only family class disaster at Devon that was worse than ours occurred years later when I loaned our sweet, solid, reliable white pony, Gwynedd Ask Me, to the Mutch family for little Bert to ride. Mounted on beautiful perfectly-matched white horses the Mutch family was the sure winners until the last canter when Gwynedd, who never ever bucked before or since, impolitely bucked Bert off. Luckily unscathed, Bert went on to win the Finals and to become a top professional horseman, but that was a bad day, and of course, I felt terrible.

Then there were some years at Devon when I was an also-ran and Carol won on her wonderful little horse, "The Kitten." The little girl on the little horse, they skipped around the courses, winning everything in sight. The judges loved them, and it was no wonder. Everyone likes to watch partnerships like that; they were cuter than cute, and GOOD. I, on the other hand, was lumpy and awkward. Though I rode okay and my horses were all right, there was not that charisma, but I loved the animals—I was fine with that and the sport.

My college years were good ones at Devon. Exams were over, the summer lay ahead, my boyfriend, later husband, Max, was encouraging me, and my dear Mr. Coker was jumping well enough to get ribbons there, even to win the Fault and Out once, beating the invincible Adolf Mogavero. We would drive all the way from Northampton, Massachusetts with Coker kicking the back of the two-horse trailer. In those days Smith College did not permit students to have cars. "But a car and a horse trailer?" "Well . . . okay . . ." and off we went to Devon. We always stayed at the George Washington Motor Lodge, now long gone, at King of Prussia, where I stayed this year at Motel 6, cheap and cheerful, and . . . they allow dogs.

During Max's and my early married years, Devon was always a fixture on our calendar. My job teaching high school English at Rosemary Hall School was over just in time for me to dash to Devon. I showed Coker and others all week long, and Max always came on the weekends to cheer me on. Besides Coker, my best horse then was Pushover, a racetrack reject, bred in the purple but he had serious soundness problems, mostly in his feet which were about four sizes too small for the size of his strapping, muscular body. I found a genius blacksmith at the University of Pennsylvania Veterinary School, then in downtown Philadelphia, Jack Anderson. Every month I drove the horse to Jack, a four-hour journey one way, to be shod. Pushy would walk into Jack's shop lame and walk out sound. Anyone who ever tried to walk, run, and jump in shoes or feet four sizes too small can understand the importance of good shoeing. The cost was more than my monthly salary of $300 for teaching school, but Pushy's owners, the Valentines, were enthusiastic and generous. All I had to do was get him there and back home again; they even paid me for transporting him.

Anyway, to make a long story short, Pushy proved to be a fabulous jumper—scopey, careful, fast—and if his feet hurt a little, he forgot about it in the excitement of competing. Devon was always one of his best shows, for he loved the crowd and the drama. He won some good classes at Devon over the years, and when I got pregnant, my sister Carol showed him successfully, for by then she was on the U.S. Equestrian Team. They also won classes at all the indoor shows—Harrisburg, Washington, and New York (Madison Square Garden). His owners, the Valentines, lived near Philadelphia, so they especially liked to watch him at Devon.

Our own children, Hans and Philip, were deprived of competing in the Lead Line Class at Devon, for by that time my business had grown, and I felt I had to focus my attention on my clients. The thought of trying to do right by my two young children and my riders and their horses was too overwhelming. On the other hand, our kids never had the dubious honor of showing at Devon in the Parent-and-Child class and the Family Class. Mixed memories prompted my decision not to go there.

By the late '70's our boys were old enough to show at Devon. Our first big outing was when ten-year-old Philip rode Frosty Lad in the Small Pony Hunter Classes. At the ingate we all held our breath, but Frosty just purred around the course, and though they didn't actually win any ribbons in that stiff competition, Phil's first experience at Devon was a good one. Besides the horse show he took in the midway, the merry-go-round, the Ferris wheel, and the traditional Devon fudge. For me, it was wonderful *déjà vu*.

In the '70's and '80's we parked our camper in a lot adjoining the horse show and behind the fish market. We had to keep the windows closed for the stench from the fish market was stifling. We also had to keep the curtains drawn for Mike, the "were-wolf" we called him, was always spooking around the campers. He owned the fist market and the lot where we parked our camper. "*Where* is he now?" was often the question. Rain or shine, the fan/air conditioner ran full-blast, but it was very handy to have our "house" so close to the horse show!

The years slipped by quickly, and soon both boys were showing in the Junior Jumper Division over fences as high at 4'6". Their mounts were Bay Bullet and Little John, two trusty steeds, not world-class winners, but safe and reliable and well able to win a few ribbons, even at Devon.

By the time the '80's came along, Devon was a qualifying horse show. Riders had to amass points in other horse shows all year long in order to compete at Devon. Philip and his Wyoming Thoroughbred Sasquatch, who was as wild as his Indian name suggests, managed to qualify for the Junior Jumper Division and to be quite competitive when they got there. One year, '86 or '87, they won a really big class. Since then, showing only occasionally, Phil never, until this year, managed to qualify again.

Devon is perhaps the only prestigious horse show that insists horses and riders qualify for most divisions but leaves the door wide open for ambitious Equitation riders who want to compete against the very best in the country. All the Equitation classes, in which the rider's style, seat and control of the horse are judged, are available to any Junior rider who can jump around a 3'6" course. For years this has been a real boon for trainers like me who brought good-riding kids on medium horses in an effort to raise their sights. An important corollary was that even non-horsy parents could see that their child needed a better horse to be competitive at the highest level. At Devon talented kids without money were inspired to work harder to gain opportunities in the sport, largely the chance to ride some good horses and compete in big horse shows. In the '80's and '90's some of my students' parents did step up to the plate and buy some first-class horses, and to my delight I found it was much easier to win with good horses.

Since I was actively buying and selling horses, I was lucky to trip over a couple of really good inexpensive ones. I bought my very best horse, Johnny's Pocket, from the father of a college classmate. An American thoroughbred, he was the horse of a lifetime. By then inundated with family, farm, and clients, I felt I could not give him the ride he deserved, so I handed him over to Norman Dello Joio, at that time a talented, up-and-coming rider.

Winning the Grand Prix of Devon in 1981 was a highlight early in their career that heralded many other highlights in the years to follow. The class was traditionally held on Thursday night that year it was pouring rain and the ring was a sea of mud. Worried about the rain, the mud, the lights, and the crowd, we debated whether to show Johnny or not; was he up for it all? Though inexperienced, he proved that night to be a real pro, splashing through the mud to jump a clear round over a huge course. On to the jump off against the clock. Five other horses were clear, and several were very fast. Johnny and Norman were last to go, left out strides between the jumps, turned inside of where the others had turned and won, a thrilling moment. It was the first "huge" of many victory gallops for Norman and Johnny. After washing, drying, and blanketing our treasure, we wrapped his legs, fed him his dinner, and then retired to Martini's our favorite hangout to celebrate and enjoy a late supper. Now gone, Martini's was the watering hole of choice at Devon where for years we either celebrated or drowned our sorrows, depending on the luck of the day.

An unexpected fringe benefit of Johnny and Norman's success was that they attracted other good horses and riders to our establishment which grew in the '70's from a six-horse, four-acre plot in Greenwich to fifty-plus horses, on a one-hundred-acre farm in Bedford. During the late '70's, the '80's, and '90's a succession of good horses and riders enjoyed success at the prestigious Devon Horse Show.

Among the best was Just for Fun, an aptly-named conformation hunter who was Grand Hunter Champion at Devon one year, an accomplishment that helped assure his induction into the National Show Hunter Hall of Fame. Nicknamed "The Pro" in the barn, he proved himself to be a real pro for us at Devon. Looking beautiful and standing perfectly square, with ears pricked, he easily won the model class in which the horse's conformation is judged. He went on to win most of the classes over fences where his performance, way of moving, and style of jumping were judged. Bred and raised in Virginia, the home of our nation's best hunters, "the Pro" managed to win even under our Yankee flag, beating the best horses not only from the south, but also from all over the country. His rider, a young ingénue, managed to stay out of his way and let him win. She, of course, was awed by the grandstand full of shouting spectators and the impressive ring itself with the placard over the ingate, stating clearly that Devon was "Where Champions Meet."

Just for Fun was a champion before we bought him, he was expensive, six figures, a lot in the '80's, still a lot. We figured out how to let him keep on winning which he did for us and his next owners in California, proving once again a good horse is a good horse, and as riders and trainers all we have to figure out is how to let him be good.

Now that is not always as easy as it sounds. One year I was detained at home until the night before the first class when another good and expensive horse was to show. We schooled him early in the morning, and he was awful: nervous and scared, totally not himself. "What have they, (his rider and a trainer friend,) been doing to him?" I asked myself in tears as I led him back to his stall.

"What the hell is the matter with you, crying at this hour?" barked my good friend and mentor, Dave Kelley.

"They have ruined my horse," I sobbed.

"Nonsense!" he answered. "Send him home, turn him out for a few weeks, and go again at Fairfield the end of the month," which is exactly what I did, and it worked. The horse was fine, but that was a terrible Devon for me even though my other riders and horses did pretty well.

Devon 2009 began auspiciously with Just For Fun's induction into the Hall of Fame on Tuesday evening at the historic Merion Cricket Club right on the Main Line. His California entourage was there in force—grandmother, parents, rider, and two trainers—and he was truly feted. The next highlight of the week was to be son Philip and Glasgow competing in the High Amateur-Owner Jumper Division on the weekend, Philip's first ride at Devon in over twenty years. Since he shows in only a few events all year long, he never qualified. Now Glasgow, like Just for Fun, has this habit of winning, no matter what, so it was no surprise that they won enough classes during the year to qualify for Devon at just a few horse shows. Glasgow had had a brilliant career winning all over the world with Norman Dello Joio, by then a world-class rider and good friend. A while ago Norman decided that the 1 meter 60 jumps were a bit too strenuous for the aging champion and "Would Philip like to show him in the Amateur Division?" I guess so!!!! Norman persuaded the other owners to give him to us, and 1 meter 45 looked easy to the eighteen-year-old wonder horse.

So here we were at Devon 2009, Phil for the first time in twenty years and Glasgow, recently demoted from 1 meter 60 competition to 1 meter 45; the jumps were over one foot smaller. We were ready for an exciting weekend, but it rained and it rained all week long, drumming noisily on the tin roof as we sat in the barn on our tack trunks, munching Devon fudge, and gossiping. The ring was a sea of mud. It became increasingly evident that this pair would never set foot in this ring this week, because the eighteen year old Glasgow was spared the inconvenience, the indignity, and the danger of wallowing in the mud for a little glory and money. On Thursday and Friday we scratched, and solemnly watched the others struggle around the impossibly muddy track. Surveying the ring Friday night, I thought, "No Way," but I was wrong . . . luckily.

Saturday dawned sunny and breezy. The jump crew had worked all night siphoning the ankle-deep water off the ring, and by morning the footing looked okay. By noon it was ideal, and we got ready to show in the $15,000 Classic, the big class of the week.

In the schooling area that morning when it became evident we could show, Norman devised a simple, slow, little exercise with rails on the ground to calm everyone's nerves and to practice looking early for the next rail/jump, very important for an amateur rider like Phil who fares better in big open fields than in small rings where the jumps come up fast. Devon is by no means a small ring, but it seemed so to Phil who is used to showing in wide open spaces. We felt confident and ready.

The course walk just before the class put us on notice that this was no small event. The jumps were huge, many of them off sharp turns, and the distances between the jumps challenging—demanding that the rider regulate the horse's stride with the horse obediently complying. Norman and Philip carefully paced off the distances and mapped out a plan. Our post position was lucky; we went 15th, so we had a chance to watch several horses go before warming up, clearly an advantage in a technical course like this one.

The course seemed to ride exactly as planned. The warm up in the schooling area went well. First, an oxer that was small to start with, then bigger and bigger. Finally they finished over a tall 5' vertical to let Glasgow know there would be big jumps in the ring. Phil rode the course exactly as planned, and Glasgow jumped brilliantly, a clear round, and they qualified for the jump off against the clock. The jumps were raised, and the six who jumped clear rounds were eligible to jump off. We went fourth in the order, warmed up again, watched a couple and Norman calmly said, "You have to leave out a stride after the double, five, not six strides to the Liverpool. Don't overdo, he will get there easily, then gather him and patiently jump that tall, careful vertical, and leave out a stride to the last oxer. Let him lengthen, don't overdue, and for God's sake don't push him through the front rail of that last oxer.

Meanwhile, I was thinking of our friend Michael's words, "Stay out of his way. Let him jump a clear round." Phil did just that and they sped around the course, easily leaving out a stride at the Liverpool, calmly turning to carefully jump the vertical planks on flat cups, and finally slipping along and over the last massive oxer. Clear in the fastest time, however there was one more to go, a "Rabbit" as it were, that had beaten us the summer before in a big class. We all stood at the ingate with our hands in our left pockets, an old racetrack superstition, for luck. They had the time, but luckily the rider got excited at the last jump and pushed the little horse through the front rail of the oxer. "Hooray! We Won" Lots of hugs, crying, etc. Glasgow was calmly standing by waiting for Phil's leg up to go into the ring for the presentation. Probably he was thinking, "This is nice, but compared to the King's Cup in Hickstead, England, (the Queen herself presented it), and the President Cup in Washington, this is kind of a country show, but any glory is good." And all glory is fleeting. In a few minutes the presentation was over, the victory gallop around the ring was finished. We packed up and headed home, traditional Devon fudge in our bags. As I drove down Route 30, I saluted the place where Martini's used to be and thought, "This was the best Devon ever, possibly the best horse show ever." Wins like that are almanacked; no one can ever take them away from you.

Vince Lombardi once said: "Winning isn't everything. It is the only thing." I partly agree with him. When you win at Devon, it IS the only thing. Who was second to Glasgow and Philip. I don't know. Maybe Secretariat. Any ribbon at Devon is treasured and even to ride your best and have a good experience there, like Phil did many years ago on his small pony, is enough. And there is always the Fair and the Fudge.

Philip Richter on his small pony,
Frosty Lad, competing for the first time at
Devon in the '70's.

Glasgow and Philip Richter enjoy
The Winner's Circle at
The Devon Horse Show, 2009.

II.

Horses

Gypsy

In the 1930's my mother bought her first horse off a cattle car that came into Kansas City from somewhere out west. She looked over the fifty frightened horses waiting to be unloaded and paid a hundred dollars for the one she thought was the prettiest. A redhead herself, she particularly liked the red, chestnut mare with the white blaze down her face. Not knowing where the horse came from or where she and the horse were going, she named her Gypsy.

    She boarded the mare and rode at a riding club called the Saddle and Sirloin where a fast, young crowd gathered most evenings after work to ride, have dinner together, and party a bit. Mother had a good job as a buyer for the big department store in town, so she was quite prosperous even though it was the bottom of the Depression.

    The old saying, "Chestnut mare, beware!" applied to Gypsy. She was barely saddle broke, being allegedly three-years-old, probably two. The age of horses can be estimated by looking at their teeth, but there is some room for fudging. When they're too young, make them older, and vice versa. The two redheads cut quite a swarth through the Saddle and Sirloin and were not unnoticed by a swell, young man, later to be my father. He was, however, mostly interested in the tight, yellow sweater often worn by Gypsy's rider. He was a mere shipping clerk earning $15.00 a week working for a company back East called Johnson and Johnson. He could only afford to rent a horse now and then to join the fun.

    One thing led to another, and she bought him a horse, Fancy Nell. They married, and moved to Boston where he was promoted to be the New England regional sales manager. The horses arrived by train, and soon it was discovered that Gypsy could really rack. The rack is a very fast, single foot where one leg strikes the ground at a time. That is one of the gaits of a Five Gaited Saddle horse, a prominent American breed of horse with fiery eyes, arched neck and tails. Gypsy was a bit on the plain side by their standards, but she could rack like the wind. Before I was born my parents had a lot of fun showing in the Boston area. Years later, my sister and I saw a late version of the scene when we showed her at some county fairs in Vermont. Mother in her tight jodhpurs; Gypsy, mane and tail and legs flying, our father at ringside hollering and banging the fence to urge them on. They always won. As Gypsy flew past the fancy horses, they flustered, faltered, and broke stride. She always won, even though she was not at all fancy.

After we bought the little, old, abandoned farm in Vermont in the forties, Mother became interested in endurance competition and every year rode Gypsy in the Green Mountain Horse Association 100 Mile Trail Ride, held annually still today over Labor Day weekend. Endurance was right up Gyspy's alley in those days. She was indefatigable, and though she never won, she was always in the top 5 of 50 or 60 competitors.

As my parents' interests broadened to hunters and jumpers when we moved to our farm in rural New Jersey, Gypsy gamely learned how to jump. Most five-gaited horses do not jump at all, but Gypsy managed to figure out how to get to the other side of any obstacle put in front of her. Her experience as an endurance horse helped her navigate the cross country jumps, for she was used to trotting and cantering over rough terrain. Being sure-footed helped her jump ditches, logs, stonewalls, chicken coops, and even the tall, split rail fences that criss-crossed the New Jersey countryside; never a scopey, airy jumper she just did what she had to do: jump the jumps. Our ages not far from the double digits, (10 years), my sister and I were keen to ride, and since there was only one pony, one of us rode Gypsy when we rode together. Then our pony broke her leg and had to have a year off, so Gypsy's job was doubled, but she soldiered on.

For comic relief she and mother continued their old game of longeing without the longe line. Longeing is a method for exercising horses without riding them. To longe a horse you need a long rope and a long whip. The horse goes around the person standing in the middle of the circle. Gypsy's game was to jog around Mother with no rope attached to the halter. But the real fun part was when Mother shook the whip at her. Gypsy would charge at her and narrowly miss running her over. For us kids it was scary to watch, even though we knew it was just a game and Gypsy would never harm our mother. No one else was ever brave enough to play that game with Gypsy.

Sometimes Gypsy was pressed into service to go fox hunting. A family of four, three really, my father was too big to ride Gypsy, needed a couple of horses each, sound in wind and limb, to fox hunt regularly; my mother, three days a week, my sister and I on Saturdays. If one of our steeds were lame or sick, Gypsy would have to "carry us to hounds." Whoever rode her could not go "first flight," tin canning over all the tall, split rail fencing, so popular in New Jersey and other hunting counties across the nation. Gypsy and her rider would join the "hill toppers," the people who tried to out fox the fox, take short cuts, and most importantly avoid the bigger fences at a fast pace. Gypsy fit into that crowd just fine and was a patient, docile leader or follower, understanding in her own way that "hill topping" was a good thing for her.

One of Gypsy's many tasks was to be our "guest horse;" theoretically the guest horse is a safe conveyance for visiting friends and relatives. Our cousins from Iowa and elsewhere have some vivid memories of Gypsy. As kids we were expected to take care of the horses as well as ride them. Gypsy had a few foibles that were scary for people not used to horses. While she was eating her grain, no one was allowed in her stall. She would simply bare her teeth and chase you out. She was also cinchy; she hated having her girth tightened abruptly when you saddled her, and if you were too rough, she would try to rip your arm off. Riding her, you had to be careful not to rile her up. To the end of her days she was a quirky, red-head and had to be handled carefully; what worked best was not bug her. That was also the best way to get along with our mother and a lot of other people we've encountered since.

My cousins' fondest memories of Gypsy were the jolly rides in the cart. Yes, besides everything else, she knew how to pull a wagon or a cart. She was so calm the first time we hitched her up that it seemed quite likely she learned about driving in a previous lifetime, perhaps as a youngster before her ride East to Kansas City in the cattle car. The notion of hitching any of our other fractious horses was out of the question, so once again the job fell to Gypsy. She cheerfully acquiesced, and we had a lot of fun driving around the countryside. Oddly enough as pre-teens we were too young to drive a car, but we could go anywhere with a horse and cart, important for kids stranded on a farm miles from anywhere. A favorite destination was the country store several miles away where one of us would stay with Gypsy outside while the other went in for popsicles and Cokes for all, even the horse.

Our favorite sport with Gypsy was getting her to "rack on," a game undertaken when Mother was off the farm. Our little fox hunting friends knew nothing about gaited horses (neither did we, except how to get Gypsy

Gypsy is racking to victory in the early 1940's,
"Rack On!

Gypsy is pulling the cart full of Hofmann cousins.

to rack), and were fascinated by her flying gait, as fast as a gallop. The track around the neighbor's red barn was perfect for these escapades. It took a little kicking and snatching to get her going, but you could hear her coming before she actually flew by the chorus of kids shouting, "Rack on. Rack on!" It was almost as much fun to incite the crowd as to ride the fiery thunderbolt round and round. In the early days Gypsy had enough fire in her belly that everyone could have a turn. As the years slipped by, she was smart enough to trot quietly no matter how much we kicked and shouted. The excitement of that game was over.

As Gypsy approached the age of forty and became increasingly arthritic, my mother made the tough decision to have her put to sleep. Her demise foreshadowed the end of our childhood as well as the end of our parents' youth. The reign of the redheads was over. It was the end of an era.

Who is Lady Ardmore Anyway?

One day when the family was gathered in the kitchen, our granddaughter, Margot, then age six, asked impatiently, "Who is Lady Ardmore anyway?"

Margot knows all the horses in our barn by name and can even tell the look-alikes apart. She was also subtly boasting to us that she could read the tarnished plaque under Lady's portrait. Not bad for six-years-old. Lady, OK. But Ardmore? What is that?

Remembering how when I was her age, my grandmother used to bore us with her long-winded explanations about the various memorabilia in her vast Victorian house in Ottumwa, Iowa, I tried to summarize briefly who and what Lady Ardmore was, saying,

"She was our first really good horse. She taught us that big fences are easy and fun to jump, that anything was possible."

"Then why didn't you name the farm after her?" Margot doesn't miss any nuances; she knows you name your farm after your first good horse.

"Well, actually," I explained, "she was my mother's horse, and their farm already had a name. But she used to let us ride her sometimes. I rode her in my best horse show ever in 1952 when I was thirteen, and we won every single class, Best Horse in Show, and Best Child Rider. It was 'huge,' as people say today."

"Wow," said Margot, who usually is not easily impressed.

I did not elaborate, and we were on to other stuff. The portrait of Lady had been merely wallpaper in our kitchen ever since my mother died and left me the lovely CW Anderson pastel. I had not thought about Lady in years. She suffered from "the ingratitude of children;" I never until now appreciated what she did for us—my parents, my sister, Carol, and myself. Prompted by Margot, I fell to reminiscing about the hot, bay Thoroughbred mare my parents bought in the late '40's for $100 off the Empire Race Track, a two-bit track located in the back of Brooklyn.

Ludi Stadtmueller, our blacksmith and good friend, found her, a four-year-old mare with a bowed tendon. The owners figured she was worthless, only going to cost them money, and gave her to her groom. The outfit was moving on, and the groom could not afford to ship her to the next town, wherever that was, probably Finger Lakes in upper New York State.

"She's bred in the purple," Ludi enthused. "Her uncle is Man O'War . . . ." In those days every Thoroughbred horse was allegedly related to Man O'War. "Her grandfather, Fair Play, was Man O'War's father. Here are her papers," and he pulled her wrinkled Jockey Club Registration out of the pocket of his dirty jeans. At that time, registration papers went wherever the horse went. Now race horse owners hang on to them for fear the buyers will improve the horse, run it back, and beat their horses. Today cheap Thoroughbreds stay off the track and find jobs elsewhere or go to the glue factory. Most show horse owners are keen to know a horse's breeding in case there is some good jumping blood, but particularly in the case of the geldings, they are not adamant about the papers, per se. Anyone can turn the upper lip inside out to read the horse's tattoo and track down his breeding on the Internet. The Jockey Club, responsible for the registration of all American Thoroughbred horses, is dialed in. Even I, rather computer impaired, can look up a horse's breeding.

Ludi was adamant. "She's a good'un, but she needs time. She has to have a year off before you can ride her. Then she'll be right as rain."

A year off! To pre-teens that was an eternity. To our mother, the eager horsewoman, that was an awfully long time, and to our father, used to instant, hop-to gratification, that was forever. But Ludi was firm.

"If you can't wait, leave her there," he admonished.

They went to see her, fell in love with her and my father peeled off five twenties and handed the money over to the hungry groom. She gamely limped into our dark, makeshift two-horse trailer and gave one lonesome whinny as we drove away from her friends in the tumble down shed row. That's how the horse that was to teach us so much came into our lives.

Our eminent neighbor, Arthur McCashin, who had recently been anointed captain of the fledging, civilian US Olympic Show Jumping Team, had lots to say on the subject of the new horse from the dealer's point of view.

"You guys are stupid. They go lame soon enough. You don't buy a lamer . . . ." Well, we already owned her, and we gave her a year off. My mother trained her, and she was not bad: hot, flighty, but OK. She "rode her to hounds," as the saying goes, at least twice a week. The mare had "no bottom," i.e., she never got tired. That was a good thing in a family like ours because she got ridden a lot and jumped hundreds of fences every week.

The summer of '52 Lady was mine. My mother went off to Europe to watch Arthur win an Olympic medal in Helsinki. I trained Lady rigorously all summer. (Like I said, she had no bottom; she could take it.) The Woodstock Horse Show was a fixture on our calendar, and I made sure we were ready, and as I had told Margot, we won everything. I think we did seven or eight classes that day. Now people are horrified if you show in more than one or two.

And so life went on. Lady went fox hunting with Mother, pony clubbing, horse showing, and racing with us. We used to ride down to McCashin's when the Olympic hopefuls trained, and we jumped all their jumps, even the giant Irish bank. There was nothing Lady could not do . . . and Arthur hated her . . . "that hot Thoroughbred mare." He finally laid off the bowed tendon that by then was healed and crabbed about her "mule feet." Well, she did have mule feet, narrow and contracted, but they worked for her . . . . She stayed sound as a dollar, and we just kept on riding and jumping her.

Lady never stopped feeding our egos, giving us confidence, or whatever you want to call it. The experts down the road said she was no good, but every week she was beating them at the horse shows. Mind you, by now she was a seasoned campaigner, and often the McCashin steeds at the shows were fresh off the boat from Ireland and green as grass. What did we care? We beat them.

If you are winning, criticism bounces off. You hear it, but it is not devastating. My mother came back from Helsinki, sprinkled with Medal dust, and she scolded me when she saw the Woodstock win picture: no hairnet. She was right, of course, but I had won anyway, hairnet or no hairnet. (Maybe that's why I've always considered time in the hair dressers, the beauty parlor, wasted time. I don't go there. I'd rather be riding.) Mother's other quibble was the severe double bridle. The curb bit kept Lady under control. She knew it was there and did not even try to run away . . . .

The years rolled by and Lady kept jumping bigger and bigger fences. No problem. Sister Carol rode her a lot then, even trained at the US Equestrian Team Center, under the renowned *chef d'equipe* Bert de Nemethy. "The Lady" was not intimidated by the big jumps, the famous trainer, and the

Lady Ardmore.
This portrait by C.W. Anderson is such
a good likeness she could turn and look at you.

Lady Ardmore and the Author
at the Woodstock Horse Show in 1952.

awesome venue. She just galloped and jumped like always, so Carol relaxed and rode her well. Good old Lady gave her the audacity to hop on to the Olympic Squad and horse show all over Europe.

Lady grew old gracefully, gamely jumping lower and easier fences. Her old bones made her feel like a *Mercedes* with the air gradually going out of its tires. Everything that used to be effortless was becoming a struggle. We retired her, hoping she would raise a couple of colts, but she declined. Finally now, I appreciate all she did, for she literally jump-started us and showed us we could compete in the big ring. I hope if the granddaughters want to jump bigger fences, there will be a Lady Ardmore somewhere to show them it is fun and easy.

Looking at CW Anderson's portrait of her hanging in my kitchen, I see that it was such a good likeness, she could turn and look at you. The artist loved the Man O'War line and captured her spirit in his pastels. She was a lovely type: sharp little ears, finely chiseled face, wise, kind eye. I remember as if it were yesterday, the day he came to see her at our farm in Vermont. A sandy-haired, ordinary-looking man, he politely entertained us drawing pictures while mother served lunch. We knew he was a famous artist and were surprised he was not at all unusual. After lunch, he simply sat alone in the corner of Lady's stall and watched her pick at her hay. He made a few sketches but took no photos. In our pre-teen estimation his visit was essentially a non-event. Because he knew her only in her stall, he never saw "the look of eagles" when her blood was up, so he portrayed the confident, calm Lady at rest. She was not great, but she was surely good to our family. She put us on the map when we did not even know there was a map.

Even today, some people think we are "backyardy," provincial, and sometimes we are. Like going to the jumps, any decision, even the wrong one, is better than no decision. Lady gave us the courage to be decisive. Lady and many other horses in my life reconfirm my belief that learning to ride horses is good for little girls, and hence I urge parents to give their daughters riding lessons. Choices of womanhood are indeed "given" by the horse. Horses do the same for boys if they have the grit to withstand being beaten sometimes by girls. If not, they get their confidence elsewhere: on the football field, or the baseball diamond, or the hockey rink.

Lady's legacy is that the experts know a lot and should be listened to, but at the end of the day trust your horse and your instincts. If there is no horse, your own instincts will do.

Thanks Lady.

Who is Stacey? What is She?

Like all of us as we age, Stacey has become temperamentally more of what she was when she was young and physically less. She is a homebred bay mare, nearly twenty-years-old. Although by nature not very friendly, she has been a steadfast friend to me for a long time, often "picking up the slack" when there is slack, and right now there is slack. Her horse show name is "Pocket Change" and she is exactly that, not a "ten" anything but a good, useful horse that gives our family lots of pleasure and teaches many of my students how to be good horsemen and how to ride well.

I reconnected with her recently because I needed a capable, reliable steed for my son Hans to ride with his daughter Maxine in a three-mile cross-country Hunter Pace. No one was standing in line to ride Stacey, so the job of getting her fit fell to me, and I have enjoyed her immensely for the past several weeks.

When I saddled her the first day of our new regime, I remembered that she is what horsemen call "cinchy," i.e., she does not like to have her girth pulled up quickly. No matter how slowly and carefully you tighten her girth; she always tries to bite anyone within range. Now she has expanded her defenses to kicking as well. With the bridle she is more impatient than ever, nearly snatching the bit out of my hands, as if to say, "OK. Let's get going."

Mounting her has always been easy unless you dilly-dally. She would stand like a rock anywhere: by the mounting block, car bumper, a tree down in the woods, but be sure not to take more than thirty seconds to get on, or she'd leave without you. She would definitely leave without you if you flop clumsily on her back. One of the many lessons she taught my working student Greg one winter was how to mount properly, a very important lesson, for "well begun is half done." He learned not to jab his left foot into her ribs, but to put it gently against the girth. With his reins gathered in his left hand, he was able to put his right hand on the pommel, the front of the saddle, to balance himself as he swung his right leg over her back and found the right stirrup. Standing in his irons, he would slowly and gently sink into the saddle as she moved off. For years she has helped me teach. Like most of my students now, human and equine, she does it my way, but better than I could at this point. She expects everyone to be considerate of her needs and her foibles as well. For example, when she bangs on the paddock gate it is not always easy to distinguish the need from the foible. In any case, the message is clear; she wants to come in to her stall NOW. It is possible the flies are biting and annoying her, but it is more likely that she has simply decided she's had enough in the field. Another consideration is that it might be almost suppertime, and she certainly does not want to risk missing a meal.

When I started riding her this fall, I had forgotten how lovely and long her neck is. For some reason a horse with a "lot out in front of you," long neck and big shoulders, is easier to ride than a stubby, short-necked creature. Especially tall, long-waisted people have trouble staying behind short-necked horses; you feel that you could easily fall off over the front.

Stacey has beautiful, natural balance and carries herself lightly across the ground at all three gaits: walk, trot, and canter, and especially at the gallop she is a lovely, light, and airy ride. We've been doing a lot of galloping around the back fields to get ready for the Hunter Pace which happens mostly at the gallop.

Horses that lack natural balance are often built "down hill," hindquarters higher than their shoulders or "strung out," hind legs traveling behind them instead of under them. Such horses need considerable help from the rider, mostly kicking the rear end under them with their legs while supporting the front end with a hold on the reins.

Stacey does not need a helpful, intrusive rider and that's a good thing because she won't put up with one, not even a little bit. She has a lovely, soft, almost fussy mouth, and a heavy-handed grabber makes her furious, shaking her head and trying to tear the reins from his hands. Likewise, her reaction to a kick in her ribs is swift and sudden. In lessons I tell her riders to "think trot and she will." Another important maxim she taught Greg was to be "light in the tack," not like a "sack of potatoes" on her back. A clumsy, heavy, insensitive and/or inexperienced rider "hots her up" in a heartbeat.

Over the years she has become more intolerant of bad riders, partly because she's endured some insensitive riders but mostly because she is just "over it." It is interesting that a rider's weight is not necessarily a factor. Hans, who weighs in at about 200 pounds "rides light;" she likes him better than fussy, light-weights or heavy-riding middle-weights.

Stacey is not only cranky; she is bossy as well. Surprisingly she has had the same boyfriend for well over a decade. Reggie, an Australian Thoroughbred who is now living on his third continent, having passed through Holland on his way to America and who has reached the venerable age of twenty-six, is devoted to her. He has seen it all and loves her the best. They are inseparable; they share a stall, for even if they are in adjoining stalls, they scream for each other incessantly. If one goes out to be ridden, the other hollers until he or she comes home. Poor old Reggie nearly died of a broken heart when Stacey was off having her foals. Their reunions after long separations, whether child rearing or horse-showing, were always touching. Their snufflings, "how ARE you, dear?" could bring tears to your eyes. Short separations like an hour's ride nowadays can end differently, for she will sometimes snap at him if he makes too much of a fuss over her when they are reunited.

Most horsemen prefer geldings over mares, for as a rule like dear Reggie, their temperaments are steadier; and they will put up with more. However, a good mare in the right hands can be as good as or better than any gelding or stallion. That is why we see more mares at the top of our sport than at the bottom. They will not tolerate the insensitive and the inexperienced. Two gold-medal winning, show jumping combinations were little "Touch of Class" ridden by Joe Fargis in the '80's and "Halla" with Hans Winkler in the '50's, the latter carried her rider around despite his pulled groin muscle, or as Hans put it "because of it." He had no choice but to stay out of her way as best he could and let her jump clear rounds that day.

So "Who is Stacey? What is She?" She is a mare, as I said, not a 10 anything, not scopey enough to jump Olympic courses and catch the eye of a world-class rider. In her youth she packed me over some pretty stout Preliminary Jumper courses, and with son Philip she squeaked around in some big High Amateur Jumper classes. She has a lot of "heart" and will try her hardest to leave the jumps up.

In recent years the jumps have shrunk; it would not be fair to ask her to jump high now that she's in her late teens. Although she has always been a sound horse, she comes out a bit wooden and needs a long walk before she goes to work. Last winter she enjoyed a real renaissance under my student's guidance once he figured out how to ride her. He had ridden the summer before under the renowned Hans Winkler, so Stacey had to teach him that the domineering German "leg-to-hand" method did not work with all horses. In short, he found out "there are many roads to Rome." Yet even though every horse is different, they do fall into certain categories. For example, Stacey is no "Euro;" she is a hot, American Thoroughbred who needs a quiet, sympathetic ride.

She took four years off to raise four decent, but not splendid colts. For about five years in addition to her other chores of raising colts and teaching lessons, she carried my husband Max safely across country every fine morning. A member of the family, niece of Johnny's Pocket, our horse of a lifetime, she was from the day of her birth a keeper, and her main job lately has been to teach her many riders to be sympathetic and to listen to their horses.

Queenie and the Circle of Life

A highlight of my recent trip to Ireland was the birth of a new foal. When my friend, Eugene, sent his sister to the airport to collect me, I knew straightaway that Queenie who was due the week before had not foaled yet, and when I stepped outside the airport, I knew why. It was cold and rainy, a "soft rain" as the Irish say. When we got to the farm I made excuses for her, "No mare in her right mind would drop a foal in this weather if she could wait."

"Well, she clearly hasn't a notion, and I've enough waitin," he answered, edgy and bleary-eyed. He didn't need to tell me he'd been up every two hours since a fortnight before her due date; that's three weeks already.

I agreed to help him by taking the midnight and 2 am watch, leaving the 4 am and 6 am duty. Saturday day and night were uneventful as was Sunday. Queenie spent her days waddling around the meadow near the house, thoughtfully munching the fresh grass, greener in Ireland than anywhere else in the world.

As we checked her every few hours during the day, I pointed out to Eugene that the cold rain on her backside was only reminding her why she didn't want to foal yet.

"Ahh. She's used to it. Got to be bloody used to it if you live here."

Queenie lives and works there. And I mean works. Someone from the North of Ireland sent her to Eugene as a three-year-old to break, train, and sell. He liked her so much he bought her himself. A squat, blocky, cobby mare, she has been a solid mainstay of his business for the past thirteen years. Every spring she produces a fine, strong foal which Eugene either sells or keeps as a school horse. He has an active lesson business; all the kids in the neighborhood and beyond learn to ride with him. Queenie's foals are weaned at three months, not the usual five or six, so she can go back to work, giving two or three lessons a day.

Starting in August, Eugene fox hunts her once or twice a week for four or five hours or rents her out to wealthy visitors. She is a versatile hunter, equally capable in "the wall country" which is criss-crossed by ubiquitous, formidable stone walls, and in "the bank country" where towering banks are flanked by boggy "drains," yawning ditches, who knows how deep. (We don't want to and hope not to find out by falling into one.) Most visitors have never seen such awesome obstacles, let alone jumped any, so the horse really must know what he or she is doing, and Queenie does. Since she foals every spring, Queenie does not hunt after February 1st, but she works in the school until she is a fortnight out from her due date. Queenie has a lot of jobs, and she works hard year round. This year she is sixteen, and Eugene has decided that this will be her last foal. Maybe that's why Queenie is hanging on to it long past her due date.

In between checking on Queenie all day long, we passed the time puttering about at the farm. Built around a courtyard, the house and barns date back to the eighteenth century. The crumbling stone barns are spruced up with twenty-first-century state-of-the-art black sliding metal doors. The freshly painted yellow house features walls nearly two feet thick.

The "soft rain" did not deter us from doing the various fix-it repairs necessary after the ravages of winter. The ring fencing had some loose boards which we nailed back up, and several jumps in the ring itself needed repairs as well. I raked the courtyard while Eugene dragged the ring. In just a few hours time the place looked shipshape, but still no foal.

"She hasn't a notion," muttered Eugene as he brought her in from the field and fed her a warm bran mash for dinner.

Darkness fell, the rain continued, and there was no foal at 8 pm, 10 pm, midnight—my watch. I slept in my clothes, heathen style, so I could quickly jump out of bed when the alarm dragged me from the depths of darkness to cross the moonlit courtyard to Queenie's stall. I could see the white star on her forehead, as she thoughtfully gazed at the full moon behind me. I wondered when that little foal would want to leave that dark, still place where we are before we're born and after we die. All was quiet; no foal yet so I slipped back into my dark, warm bed. Two am was my watch again and I dimly heard Eugene at 4 am. When he went out at 6 am, there was the foal standing and nursing. Queenie did it all herself as she often does.

As the watery sun rose, he led the mare, with the foal wobbling along behind, across the courtyard, and banged on my bedroom window.

"Look who's here. She's only just arrived." I threw on my jacket and dashed out to welcome the newcomer. She stood quietly on shaky legs as we petted and admired her. She was bay/brown with a star on her forehead and no white legs at all; the spitting image of her mother.

"Looks like a princess to me," I said.

"She does indeed favor the mother. But we have so much royalty already—Queenie; her son Prince; King; the show jumper; Duchess the dog . . . . And now Princess?"

"Princess," I answered, somewhat teary, thinking of the dark place from whence she came, leaving behind Max, my husband, Eugene's young wife and daughter, and countless other loved ones.

"The circle of life," murmured Eugene and added, "Time for breakfast. Let's put them away. I'm hungry. Aren't you?"

Just for Fun:
His Induction into The National Show Hunter Hall of Fame

Just for Fun, a bay gelding by Keelo, was an American Thoroughbred bred by Delmar Twyman in 1980. Kenny and Sallie Wheeler, also southerners, bought him as a three-year-old and launched his brilliant career at the Warrenton Horse Show in Virginia where he won all his classes in the three-year-old division, ably ridden by Charlie Weaver.

As a four-year-old Just for Fun won 17 championships and one reserve in the First Year Green Conformation Division. With Charlie in the irons, Justin, as he was affectionately known, was Grand Hunter Champion three times in five years and garnered AHSA Horse of the Year titles in '81, '83, and '85 in the Green and Regular Conformation Hunter divisions.

Charlie had special respect for Justin, saying "He was a beautiful little horse with perfect, clean, tidy legs," and asserted that "he was a real over-achiever, he tried really hard. He jumped well, despite being under the mark in terms of stride and scope. He made the most of his good jumping style; he learned to be aggressive. He tried to win every time he walked into the ring."

As the jumps got bigger and his job got more difficult, he got tougher. He had to work at it and he was willing to do it. Junior Johnson who took care of him in those days called him "The Pro," and to me that is what is most special about that horse. He always did his best; he wanted to win.

My client, Howard Kaskel, bought Justin in 1985 for his daughter, Lauren, and "The Pro" kept right on winning for us northerners, Grand Champion at Devon with Lyda Beigel aboard and later at Fairfield with Molly Ashe-Cawley, Champion in Madison Square Garden with Charlie Weaver.

In 1987 he caught the eye of Californians Carleton and Cindy Brooks, who chose him for their owners Joseph and Patricia O'Connell and showed him for many years with tremendous success, including the 1988 AHSA Regular Conformation Hunter Horse of the Year award.

In 1992 Justin went out on top, Champion at Delmar, with Cindy aboard, and then retired shortly thereafter at the 1992 Menlo Charity Horse Show after carrying the O'Connell's granddaughter, Kate, safely in the lead line. In the Wheeler stable, the horse known as "The Pro," was indeed a real pro.

One of the last great American thoroughbred Show Hunters, Justin won for Southerners, Yankees, and Californians. Though all of us associated with him did our best to help out, he was himself; he always tried hard, and won for himself, a true champion.

Glasgow: A Great Horse

Glasgow, our two-time Olympic hopeful, who has won Grand Prix all over the world against the best in the world, qualifies as being an old/new friend. Nearly ten years ago Norman Dello Joio, world-class rider and long-time colleague, found Glasgow in Scotland and persuaded a group of us that the horse was a must-have which indeed he proved to be. For years, Glasgow won every cup around from the King George Cup in England to the President's Cup in Washington. This year for Glasgow the meter-sixty jumps were a bit of an effort, and instead of squeezing the last big jump out of the old boy, Norman opted to persuade the partners to give him to my son Philip to show occasionally in the meter-forty-five Amateur Owner Jumper classes. Mind you, Glasgow could have been sold for several hundred thousand dollars as an amateur horse, but having won nearly a million dollars he did not owe anyone anything. Among the partners were several hard-nosed businessmen who proved once again to be good-hearted horsemen. They wanted Glasgow to have an easy life with good care, and they understood how a great horse, even a good horse, actually any horse, can brighten your life, and having recently lost Max, we needed just that.

 This great horse already brightened our lives long before he set foot in the show ring under our flag. In the barn and under saddle, he is always calm and agreeable, truly a pleasure to be around and a treasure to ride. The job of keeping him fit, so he could continue to compete successfully fell to me, and starting the day was easy when I had a date to ride Glasgow at 8 am.

 The difference between a good horse and a great horse is clear to anyone who spends a little time in the saddle, but it is hard to define. Certainly, athleticism, good balance and the ability to jump big jumps is part of the package. The desire to leave the jumps up, to put enough effort into each

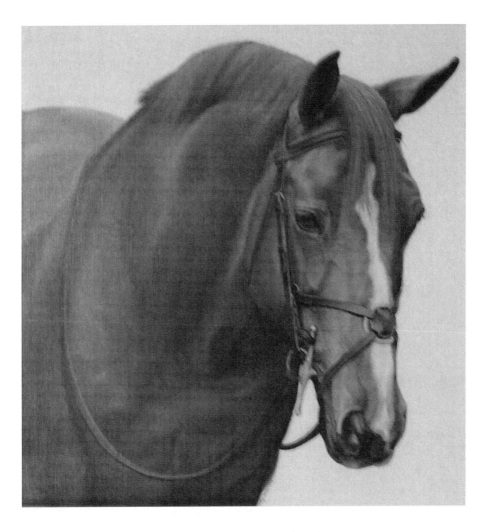

Glasgow has The Look of Eagles.
The portrait is by Jocelyn Sandor.

jump, but not to over jump is key. An even temperament, and ability to focus, and, for lack of another word, intelligence are all evident in a great horse, whether you hack him alone in a dusty ring at home or jump in Tampa Stadium where the fans are screaming for him to go clean. To be blessed with one in a lifetime is a gift from the gods, and I've been lucky to have had several. Having one great horse makes you eager for another, but filling Glasgow's shoes will not be easy for any horse.

Blink: A Keeper

After forty years in the horse business buying and selling hundreds of horses, I found out recently that I was still not immune to hanging on to a "keeper," a horse that I could have sold for a lot of money and chose not to. Born and bred in Argentina, Blink was imported to this country as a two-year-old by a little, old lady who should not break and ride two-year-olds. Unscathed, she managed to get him started, thanks to his kindly disposition, but then she decided he deserved a chance to be all he could be. Brands all over his hindquarters attested to his fine *Selle-Francais* breeding. Whoever branded him really botched the job; the brands are surrounded by unsightly scars. The poor horse must have suffered, but his affability prevailed, and he forgave us humans for abusing him so cruelly.

Purchasing another horse was not really in our budget at that time, but Max's Alzheimer's forced us to sell his airplane. The ink was barely dry on the check for the plane when I began to see the possibility of buying this horse with part of that money. We both well knew that a quality horse always improved the fullness of our already bountiful lives. I named the creature Blink, for I had just finished Malcolm Gladwell's book of that name. I had a good feeling about this unproven youngster, and over the years he has fulfilled many of my expectations. He is a good horse, not great, but good.

Max sort of understood Blink was a stand-in for his beloved, now gone, airplane. Blink's quiet, gentle disposition made him a safe conveyance for my husband on our traditional morning rides over the trails surrounding our farm after we agreed his car was as untrustworthy as his airplane. Somehow knowing that he carried precious cargo, Blink picked his way carefully over rough terrain and never shied at squirrels, deer, or dogs that would jump out of the underbrush and startle most horses. Maybe Blink was preparing himself to participate one day in Pegasus, our local program for handicapped riders when he is too old to skylark around the countryside and/or jump big fences in the show ring.

Meanwhile Blink's education as a show jumper was proceeding on schedule. His agreeable disposition enabled me to do a lot of the basic groundwork with him. He quickly learned to do balanced transitions on the flat and not to be surprised by sudden and sharp turns between the jumps. Soon he was smoothly negotiating courses of low jumps with me, and several times a week I enlisted the aid of a "real rider" to school him over higher jumps. At the horse shows, with a good rider aboard, he proved to be scopey and brave, jumping big tracks with ease, but he was not as careful as we had hoped. Sometimes he would just toe the easiest most vanilla jump, knocking it down to our great disappointment.

Because he was so generous and brave, he was a likely mount for an ambitious but untalented rider. As luck would have it, he caught the eye of a rich, no-talent who offered me a lot of money for him, like in the six figures. She ruins at least one or two horses a year, clashing her aids and sending mixed signals: "go, no don't go, GO." Sooner or later, depending on their tolerance, her horses refuse to go at all. Suddenly Blink became a keeper; I did not want to watch that happen to him, no matter what the profit, which could have been considerable. I knew I could nickel and dime along even in these tough times. I have done that before. I could take in more boarders, teach more lessons, judge more horse shows, give more clinics, and sell some cheaper horses. Luckily this farm is a money magnet; lots of people like to ride here, and even if they can't afford it, they find a way . . . and so will I.

Another reason I was reluctant to sell Blink is that he was the last horse my husband Max and I bought together. When I first saw the tall, handsome, brown colt as a four-year-old, I thought he was a promising, young show jumper and his big, calm eyes mirrored his kind heart. I use him for lessons, and lease him out for horse shows to decent riders who want to jump a bigger track. Because he is so classically correct, he is a useful "stunt horse," first horse in the ring for a rider who needs to get a good feel of the course before riding his "real horse," the one who wants to win and leaves all the jumps up. And there is always a chance that Blink will accidentally jump a couple of clear rounds and win a big class . . . .

The wise, old, groom Will Harbut, who took care of Man O'War many years ago, said it well: "A lot o'men gots a million dollars, but only one man gots Man O'War." And so it is today, reminiscent of forty years ago when Max and I opted not to sell our beloved Johnny's Pocket when we really could have used the money to buy the farm and educate our children. We did all of that and managed to keep the horse. Millions are dwindling all around us, but I still have Blink and I'm happy he is here. Now there is less pressure to sell: no mortgage for the farm and no kids to educate. Every day that starts with an 8 am ride on Blink whether jumping in the ring or trail riding around the countryside is a good day for me.

III.

The West

A Ride on a Cutting Horse

The highlight of a recent trip out west was to ride a real cutting horse. My friend's neighbor, Phil, is at the cutting edge, as it were, of that business/sport. Cutting cattle on the range is still today a serious business; how else are you going to separate the steer you want from the herd where he wants to be? Cutting cattle is also a highly competitive sport at the rodeos. Phil, our cowboy friend, still wins a lot even though he is in his late sixties.

Tall, lean, and lanky, Phil is the quintessential cowboy. When we met, he politely took off his ten-gallon hat, revealing a shock of thick, grey hair. His steady, steel-blue eyes twinkled in a craggy face, weathered by hours in the saddle in all kinds of weather. His faded, blue work shirt open at the throat barely hid his bushy chest. His scarred and scratched leather belt was highlighted by a huge, silver belt buckle, also scarred and scratched. Probably he won it in some rodeo long ago or last year. His bow-legged jeans were worn and patched, and the traditional brown cowboy boots, run down on the outside heels, hadn't seen shoe polish in a long time, if ever.

My friend, Joan, had given him a heads up that we might be by, and her hunter/jumper friend from the East (me) might like to have a ride on a cutting horse.

"A quiet, old, slow one," I added, "Like what we would call 'a school horse'."

"Cheyenne will do. He's pretty quiet and easy, but first let me show you around."

His two border collies, one old and arthritic, the other young and learning the drill, stood at attention, watching Phil's every move. He sent them down to the far meadow to bring the steers up to the ring while he showed us around the farm.

The barn was unremarkable, very workmanlike, a bit shabby around the edges, but neat and clean. The horses' coats were sleek and shiny, probably more from good feed than attentive grooming. All the tack was, of course, Western: big, long shanked curb bits and monstrous saddles that looked more like armchairs than saddles. Later I fully appreciated the big horn in front of me as I settled myself into the deep, deep seat.

Most interesting was Phil's workshop, a four-car garage where he repairs everything from cars and motorcycles to saddles and bridles. He actually makes those big, Western saddles from scratch, custom built to fit the horse's back and the rider's backside, as well. He engraves the leather and silver to the buyer's specification; he is a skilled artisan.

Back in the barn, Phil handed me a saddle and bridle and sent me down the aisle to tack up Cheyenne, "the sorrel in the last stall on the right." The non-descript, little chestnut (cowboys call them sorrels) was looking intently out his back window, and I joined him to watch the dogs bring the steers up the long hill to the ring. Never have I seen such intelligent, attentive dogs. Every time a steer even thought of leaving the herd, one of the dogs was right there to keep him with the others. No wonder Phil can manage the farm all alone; he has his dogs to help him.

Saddled and bridled, Cheyenne followed me quietly to the ring where I climbed aboard him and practiced neck reining him a bit. Western horses do not work off the direct rein at all; to get one to turn you simply lay the rein against his neck on the opposite side: the left rein on the neck makes him turn right and vice versa. It's a bit like driving in England on the wrong side of the road, familiar but opposite. Cutting horses are super sensitive to rein aids and to the rider's weight. At first I felt pretty clumsy, but soon it got better. To practice sitting still and using a very light neck rein, I guided Cheyenne carefully around the ring, first at the trot, (sitting trot only, forget posting with that giant pommel in front of you) then at the canter, or as the cowboys say "the lope," and finally at the gallop.

At the far end were the cattle mindlessly nibbling the grass at the edge of the sand ring. At the near end, the end closest to the barn, were the dogs, studying my every move and wondering what the delay was.

Soon Phil decided we were ready, whatever that meant, and explained how I should let Cheyenne know the specific steer I wanted.

"Just walk toward the one you want and look at 'em. Cheyenne will do the rest. Then just hang on to the pommel and stay out of his way."

As a lifelong trainer and former rider of hunters and jumpers, I was used to being the alpha member of the partnership with my horse, directing him where and how fast to go, what fences to jump in what sequence. This partnership was totally different; when the horse understood which steer I wanted, he took over and did the rest.

Staying out of his way was more easily said than done, I soon found out. We meandered slowly toward the herd, and I chose a white-faced Hereford with a white spot on his left side. Cheyenne pricked his ears, and the next thing I knew I was aboard a thunderbolt, zigzagging back and forth across the ring, in hot pursuit of the steer one moment, and heading him off from the front, the next. The dogs' job was to keep the steer from running to the far end of the ring. The horse and the dogs kept him bouncing back and forth across the middle of the ring and trying his damnedest to get back to the safety of the herd. Cheyenne made sure there was no chance of that.

After a few minutes, Phil said, "OK. Enough," and the horse and dogs stopped in their tracks to let the steer go back to his friends. After resting a few minutes which I sorely needed, for I was breathless, we gave it another go. This time I chose a Black Angus, quicker and meaner than the Hereford. Cheyenne was able for him, and I clung to him like a burr. Since I was used to being the alpha member of the team, I thought it would be hard not to direct the horse. But it wasn't for two reasons: first the horse knew before I did which way the steer would zigzag and second, I was too busy trying to stay on, glad for the big pommel and the deep-seated seated saddle; it would have been easy to slide off. I left the reins loose as I gripped the pommel with both hands, hanging on for dear life.

After cutting five or six cattle, I was exhausted, and content to poke around the ring and watch Phil work a promising four-year-old colt. Seeing them work, I understood that my trusty Cheyenne was school-horse-slow compared to that colt; he was like greased lightening, dodging back and forth almost quicker than I could turn my head. Soon we called it a day and sent the cattle back down to the meadow in the custody of the dogs.

Back in the barnyard we swung down off the horses, unbuckled the saddles, set them on the ground, rubbed down the horses' sweaty backs with some soft, old bath towels, and turned them into the ring, to roll in the sand, drink from the water trough and relax, before we put them up for the night and fed them their oats and hay. By the time we had stowed the tack and the horses, the dogs were back, with their panting, smiling, thirsty faces. Phil filled a pail with fresh, cold water for them and was reminded that he too was thirsty. He pulled a few "cool ones" from the fridge in the tack room, and we sat on the cement stoop by the barn, drank the beer, and watched the sun set. Another day of fun with the horses was over, very different yet in many ways, the same. Horses are horses, and horse people are horse people, no matter what they do together. On further reflection, I realized riding a cutting horse was really not all that different from riding a show jumper, for once he understands where to go and what fences to jump, the rider has to sit still in the middle of him, stay out of his way, and let him clear the obstacles as best he can.

We reluctantly drove home, waving to the tall, bow-legged cowboy, soon obscured as darkness descended.

Wyoming:

Prologue

Despite my misgiving my first vacation without Max turned out to be fun thanks to good friends who met me there, and thanks also, not surprising, to the horses that brightened my life on the ranch in Wyoming, just as they do at home.

After a long, arduous flight I landed in Cody, the cow-town I expected, rented a car, and headed out into the mountains. The vast mountain ranges, the overwhelming open space, and the endless blue sky were intimidating, but I soldiered on. As I came over Dead Indian Pass, Sunlight Valley lay beyond in the glorious afternoon sunlight. I drove down the switchbacks to the valley floor where I found the 7D Ranch, so named for the seven members of the Dominick family. When I turned down the farm lane, half a dozen horses and mules were hanging over the fence to greet me, and right away I knew I would be okay. The awesome landscape already felt friendlier as I stroked the horses' noses.

Wrangling at the 7D Ranch

Twice a day at the 7D Ranch where we were staying, the wranglers moved fifty or sixty horses to or from the ranch about five miles cross-country to the government property they lease for grazing in the summer. Every day early in the morning four wranglers rode out to bring the herd of horses, sure-footed, trusty mounts for the "dudes," back to the ranch.

Two wranglers were "pullers,"—they lead the herd and two were "pushers,"—they brought up the rear and kept the stragglers in line. In the late afternoon, 5 or 6 pm, four wranglers, sometimes the same ones, brought the horses back out to the vast, hilly, open government land. For the wranglers paying attention to "dudes" all day can get old; "wrangling," bringing the horses back and forth, was the most exciting event of the day. Even before the gates were opened, the herd of horses started restlessly moving about the corral. They knew the routine, all right, and were eager to get going. As the gates swung open at the ranch, the wranglers hollered at the horses, and they all took off at a gallop, flat out, belly to the ground, splashing through the river by the ranch and raising clouds of dust across the long, green valley to the bluffs beyond. Even those steep hills did not slow them down. We watched the fun twice a day for a couple of days, and finally the moment was right, so I asked at dinner one night if I could wrangle too.

"Dudes don't wrangle," Chuck, the ranch manager, declared flatly, "But I could check with the other wranglers. Emory says you ride OK." My friend, Emory Clark, who wrangled there as a kid was good friends with the current crew and apparently told them I was some sort of expert rider. I left it at that, and said, "Talk it over. I'd love to do it if it's OK with everyone."

The next day Chuck found me at breakfast and said I was on for the afternoon wrangle. "For God's sake, don't fall off. You're the first dude that's ever wrangled here, and we've been in business for fifty years."

"I'll try not to," I promised him, feeling the old familiar nervous knot already starting to form in my stomach.

When I used to compete in horse shows, before a major event there is always a nervous knot in my stomach from the minute I woke up in the morning (admittedly after sleeping soundly.) All day long that knot would grow, and I would gradually withdraw from the world until I got on my horse to show in the class. Then I knew I'd be fine, so I hoped the pattern would be the same with the wrangling.

"How hard can it be?" I asked myself over and over as I pretended to participate in the events of the day. A three hour ride to a picnic lunch engaged my attention as we traveled along cliff-hanger trails up and down the steep, rocky mountains that surrounded the ranch which was located in the well-named Sunlight Valley. My calm, sure-footed steed, Peso, picked his way carefully along the narrow trail as I tried to look ahead, not down at the rushing river hundreds of feet below. The eighty-four-year-old great-grandmother chattering away ahead of me kept my confidence up. She's been coming to the 7D Ranch for decades, dragging various family members along every year. She never rides between her visits to the ranch but is comfortable on her horse. From her wispy, grey hair poking out under her battered cowboy hat and her rounded shoulders to her scuffed cowboy boots, she was every inch a horse woman. I told her I wanted to be like her when I grow up.

As my first wrangle drew closer, I have to admit I don't remember much about the barbeque picnic lunch except it tasted good. Back at the ranch we unsaddled our dude horses and tacked up the wrangle horses for the run up into the mountains, the latter having a lot more "blood" than the sedate dude steeds. I was at once anxious and honored that the tall, handsome head wrangler, Chay, loaned me his own wrangle horse, a mare, Merrilegs.

"God, I hope I don't ruin her," I thought as I slung the heavy saddle over her back. The tough, wirey little horse, ears flicking, was taking in the whole scene; she knew we were getting ready to wrangle and danced around when I climbed aboard. As I settled into the deep, comfortable saddle, sure enough the knot in my stomach melted and I knew I'd be fine. I walked her around waiting for the gates to swing open and gently neck reined her and nudged her with my legs. As I expected, she was super sensitive, reacting instantly to my aids, almost as sharp as the cutting horse I rode last year. I patted her on the neck to reassure her and suddenly the gates swung open, and we were off at a brisk gallop with the thundering herd close behind.

Leggs understood right away that we were the second "pullers," she settled into the pace and did not try to overtake our leader, Chay, on a young horse who had never been the first "puller." He had warned me that Leggs and I might have to take over the lead if his colt faltered, but the youngster never missed a beat as we flew single file along the path through the woods and across the swirling river, chest high. In the valley the country opened up and we galloped, four, five, and six abreast.

"This is like fox hunting," I thought to myself, "minus the jumps and the idiots on the smart horses galloping loose beside me. Dust clouds swirling behind us, we saw the blue hills ahead radiant in the afternoon sun. Leggs galloped fast enough to stay toward the front of the herd, but she knew not to try to overtake the leader, a relief for me. I fully expected to have to wrestle her into second, for usually she was out in front with Chay in the irons.

Up and up and up through the foothills we flew, skipping over open ditches and hidden woodchuck holes. Having cracked my head badly once years ago, I was glad I had brought along my ugly brain-bucket helmet. No handsome, soft cowboy hat for me. I did not mind being the ugly oddity.

The five mile gallop twice a day had those horses fit as racehorses, and they barely drew a deep breath as we pulled up to open the gate into the government land where they would graze overnight. As they disappeared into the gathering darkness, little did we know, standing at the gate, that on the morrow they would lead us on a merry chase, the wrangle of the year, the decade, possibly the century.

Cantering back down to the ranch as the sun slipped behind the lofty mountains, we chattered companionably. The other three riders told me the names of those tall peaks that surrounded us. They enthusiastically described their lives out west and how they found their way there from all corners of the globe.

"Well this was definitely a favorite day, I thought to myself as we jogged into the yard.

The Wrangle of the Year

When my 5 am alarm clock startled me out of a deep sleep, little did I suspect that I was to be a lucky participant in "the Wrangle of the Year, "the Wrangle of the Decade," or possibly "the Wrangle of the Century." I was in the right place at the right time.

I dressed quickly in the dark and grabbed a banana to eat on my way across the yard. Coffee was not an option, for there would be no chance to pee on this long ride. That was a good decision as it turned out, for our one hour jaunt became a four hour marathon.

Outside the night was as dark as the inside of a cow. There were no lights on in any of the cabins as I stole by. Everyone was sound asleep. Munching my tasteless but filling banana, I longed for a "Katja," a coffee candy, not bitter, not sweet, that Max and I always took with us skiing.

Actually it was Max himself I was missing on this venture. He would have loved it.

There was no moon, but suddenly over the tall, distant mountains "the dawn came up like thunder." (Until that moment I never understood what they meant in that old song, "the Road to Mandalay.") All was still on the ranch, except for the horses snuffling in the corral as I passed by, heading toward the lonely, overhead light bulb shining through the door of the tack room. Chuck, the leathery, wrinkled farm manager, stepped out of the shadows, greeted me gruffly and told me which tack to bring out in the collecting area while he went to get our horses. Chay, the head wrangler, who was sleeping in that morning, had kindly loaned me his "Merrilegs" to ride again. Chuck soon reappeared out of the darkness with our two horses in tow; his big, white-faced, white-eyed "Uh-Oh" tall and snorting; my little, brown Merrilegs, quiet and calm. We tied them to the hitching rail, brushed them down, heaved up the heavy western saddles, cinched up the girths, and buckled on the bridles. Swinging into our saddles, we jogged briskly through the still, dark woods and splashed across the deep, swirling river. On the other side, Chuck took off at a gallop, with Merrilegs hot behind him. We flew along the valley and up, up and up into the hills with the summer wind tearing our eyes. At the gate where the horses were usually waiting, all sixty of them pushing and shoving each other, there was not one to be seen. As our horses gasped for breath, we scanned the hills nearby.

"Uh-Oh," said Chuck, not addressing his horse but the situation at hand. "We'll have to go find them." Easier said than done, I soon found out. We slipped through the gate and started galloping across the five thousand acres of government pasture land which the ranch leased for grazing. Now and then we stopped on the top of the bigger hills to survey the surrounding countryside. No horses. We came to a steep, wooded range of mountains on the far side of the government land.

"They must have gone up here," said Chuck hopefully.

The woods had been devastated by the forest fires of '88, and for every second growth vertical tree, there were ten horizontal trees for our horses to scramble over. I was tempted to encourage Merrilegs to jump over the logs, some of them 3' off the ground, but my little experience with western horses told me to stay out of her way because she knew what she was doing. Sure enough, she picked her way carefully and patiently through the underbrush. Meanwhile, I'm thinking, "This guy is a duffus. No herd of 60 horses would tackle these woods," but I kept quiet. Half an hour later we came to a clearing at the top of the hill. Miles and miles of rolling hills stretched out in front of us.

"They call this "the Wilderness," Chuck explained. "There's 10,000 acres of it. But our horses are not supposed to graze here." "Well-named," I thought and waited for Chuck to phone the ranch with his news—no horses at the gate, no horses on the government property they lease, and apparently the news—no horses in "the Wilderness." Chuck was starting to get anxious, for it was nearing 9 am and the tourists ride at 10.

The word from the ranch was "Call when you find them, and we'll come help you bring them in."

Chuck scanned the horizon again, and dumb like a fox, said, "I think they are behind that second hill on the left."

"Sounds good to me," I thought. "They could be anywhere," and we were off across the grassy, rolling meadows, horses' bellies to the ground. We were going much too fast to look for woodchuck holes which could send us flying head over heels, but somehow our clever horses avoided them.

Sure enough, on the back side of the second hill on the left, there they were, all sixty of them, or certainly most of them. Surprised to see us, they lifted their heads and stopped grazing to find out what would happen next.

As Chuck excitedly phoned the ranch, I was reminded of fox hunting when I was a kid with the huntsman, Buster, who used to gather his hounds and take them to the other side of the woods because he "knew" the fox was there. It always was and soon the hounds were screaming, and we were off for a good, long run through the countryside.

By the time Chuck checked that all the horses were indeed there, reinforcements from the ranch were within earshot; the sounds of horses' hooves on the hard ground and the riders' excited shouts echoed throughout the valley. We were ten miles from the ranch, so the 10 am tourist ride was pushed back to eleven and we took off.

Five cowboys came out to "help" us bring the horses back. They could not resist the fun of the wrangle of the year. Horses always know which way is home, so once we rounded them up and pushed them in that direction, little help was needed. It was easy to convince the horses to give up grazing; they had been eating all night and were also eager for adventure. Soon everyone was in full gallop, the "pullers," the two wranglers leading out in front, the herd of horses, and the "pushers" those of us behind to round up the strays. There were no strays; the horses knew where they were going

Wrangling at the 7D Ranch.
Twice a day 60 horses are moved five miles
to and from the ranch and their grazing fields.

even though the trail was not familiar to them. Chay came out also on his young horse, and I felt badly that I had kidnapped his Merrilegs that morning, but he said the big roundup was just what his colt needed, and he was off in a cloud of dust.

Knowing that there were plenty of cowboys to bring the horses in, I slowed Merrilegs to a leisurely canter, listened to the disappearing thunder of horses' hooves, replaced by birds twittering in the silent valley. Merrilegs was so smart; she did not fret to keep up with the mob, and by the time we got back to the ranch, the sweating, gasping horses were saddled for the tourists. "They will be well-behaved today," I thought to myself. "A run like that surely will take the starch of them."

I unsaddled Merrilegs, sweat still running down her legs from our run, hosed her down, and companionably grazed her under the tall trees until she was dry. Usually she would be tossed into the corral to bake dry in the sun with the others, but that day she got special "Eastern" treatment, a proper bath and cool out. Our horses would die if they were treated like these hardy, western cow ponies.

That night around the campfire there were many stories about our adventures. The hero was, of course, Chuck who somehow knew where those horses were. The worry was they would escape again across the wooded mountain range to the wilderness where they were not supposed to be. The next morning to our relief when we rode up the long hills to the gate, they were waiting for us, all sixty of them.

A Horse With A Flying Tail in Wyoming

At the ranch in the late afternoon there is usually a lull in the action around the corrals, for the tourists have finished riding for the day and are on to other activities. The evening wrangle does not happen until 5:30, so Chay, the head wrangler, uses that quiet time to work on gentling his wild horse, his current pride and joy, enthusiastically named "Champ." The chestnut stallion with a flaxen mane and tail, (cowboys call them "sorrels"), is a strapping big fellow, full-grown, about six years old, and suspicious. With a pail of grain Chay enticed him into the "round pen," a corral about 300' in diameter enclosed by a 6' fence. The horse moved as far away as possible from the gate where Chay stood.

Champ is supposedly a Missouri Fox Trotter, a breed I had never heard of before. The Internet reports that those horses are "good to pull wagons and also nice to ride" . . . that is if they will let you catch them. Chay bought this Fox Trotter a few months before at a sale over in Montana and shooed him into a truck for the ride home where he was chased into a corral at the ranch. He clearly knows Chay and watches him carefully, but he still won't let him touch him.

Chay knows he is not a magic "horse whisperer" like Monty Roberts, the showman. Every afternoon he works Champ in the round pen, standing in the center as the creature circles him, trotting and cantering. By winter he hopes to be able to put a halter on his head and lead him around. By spring maybe the horse will even let Chay ride him. The winters here are long, and deep snow will be a good ally, tiring the bronc til he gives up . . . maybe.

Meanwhile, I also tried to make friends with Champ, bringing him a carrot several times during the day as I passed his corral. In a week's time, he progressed from grabbing it off the ground after I retreated to snatching it from my hand the last day I was there, but he never did let me touch him. I had to be satisfied with that tiny triumph.

On my last day there was a tremendous triumph, of great interest to me anyway. Champ circled the round pen at a trot and then suddenly popped over the 6' fence into a neighboring corral. He cleared the high rails with ease, not even touching them. I walked over to where Champ jumped from, and the 6' fence was even higher from there. When I stood in the worn track, my hand over my head, the top rail was about where my wristwatch was, a good 6'6". Very impressive indeed. "An Olympic prospect," I thought to myself, "Too bad he won't let us touch him, let alone ride him. I wonder how may of these beasts are hiding out there in the hills."

What I do know is that I am too old to chase them down and find out. Anyway I'm sure there are plenty of show jumper riders and cowboys searching. The only bronc I know of who made it from the range to the show ring winning the King George Cup in London where the Queen awarded the prize, was Injun Joe, renamed Nautical. In the '60's Walt Disney made a splendid movie about that horse's life and called it *"The Horse with the Flying Tail."*

Injun Joe was a bronc to the end of his days. Many tried to break his spirit, but luckily no one succeeded. In the movie he was a cute palomino colt (yellow with white mane and tail) popping over little logs as he followed his mother across the prairie. Some young boys tried to corner him in a corral, but he jumped out and ran away. A succession of owners and allegedly expert trainers tried to make him obedient by beating him into submission. At a little local horse show he caught the eye of some Olympic equestrians who were intrigued by his powerful jump, and for a few hundred dollars he was theirs. A year long patient, slow program of quiet trotting and cantering in circles helped Injun Joe to be more trusting, but splitting the difference, meeting him halfway was the best way to deal with the tough, willful horse. Bert de Nemethy, the coach of the U.S. Olympic Team and a world-class horseman, spent hours trying to tame the rascal, but he understood that the horse was at his best when he did it his way. A super-careful jumper, he hated to hit the fences, and if the rider let him half run away, they would usually win. All over Europe, the crowd cheered when the wild palomino, his white mane and tail flying, plunged into the ring, and they were hardly ever disappointed. The King George Cup was just one of the many events he won here and abroad.

When I got back home I sent Chay a DVD of *"The Horse with the Flying Tail"* to inspire him to keep taming Champ. Their goal is not the Olympic Team, but to be a good wrangling team in Wyoming. Spring is in the air, and I expect that by now Champ is at least saddle broke. This is not the first bronc Chay has taught to accept a wrangler's directions, and he will do it his way.

Luckily I am not in charge of Champ; I would still be dazzled by his leap out of the corral and while feeding him carrots by the bushel, I would probably still be dreaming of making him into a world-class international show jumper, like Injun Joe.

Mentors and Protégés:
Handing Over the Reins

My clinic in Seattle the first weekend in December is becoming an annual event. After my husband died, my "children" in Seattle, now in their forties, give me "a leg up" every year. I gave them "a leg up" in the '70's when I was at the top of my game, and now at the top of their game, they have not forgotten where they came from. The special bond between a mentor and a protégé is an ongoing relationship like no other. Usually it evolves out of a shared passion: for me and mine the shared passion was and is horses and horsemanship.

When I judged a horse show out there in the '70's, one by one they came to me asking "Would you take me on as a working student?" Well, their timing was perfect; my girl wonder/working student had just been invited to train with the USET Olympic Team. "Go for it!" I said to her with huge misgivings, and suddenly there were five eager, unspoiled, unentitled kids, like a breath of fresh air from the West, to help me with the new farm. For serious riders anywhere in the US in those days, "the East" was the mecca; all the top riders and trainers and the best horses were located in the Tri-State area, the Northeast, and also in Virginia. Before the rest of the country realized they too had quality horses, we Easterners would find them while judging their horse shows or offering clinics to help them improve. We used to buy cheap and sell expensive. My best "Western" horse, Turning Point, a solid brown registered Appaloosa, was champion in Madison Square Garden. The horse world had shrunk, and everyone knows a good horse now, and many Westerners ride as well as our best Easterners.

I said, "Sure, come on out," warning them they would be sleeping on cots in sleeping bags in the cow barn, using a kitchen and bathroom next door, and worked to death. They said "Yes," and came for several summers eager to do any work in the barn and on the farm. There was plenty to do: the farm itself was rundown and overgrown, plus my business was growing like Topsy, for finally we had plenty of stalls and other amenities to attract clients. The clients generously invited the Westerners to stay in their McMansions with swimming pools and tennis courts, but the kids preferred the cow barn, and hard work on the farm, "thank you very much."

Soon we established our routine. Diminutive Cathy was my pony trainer. Thanks to her, our ponies were tuned up and won a lot at the shows. The other kids rode well enough to school clients' horses under my supervision. We worked mainly on getting those creatures obedient and easy to ride: lots of transitions in their flatwork and stride control between the jumps. Westerners were delighted to learn they could regulate their horses to do five, six or seven strides between two given jumps, a revelation for them. Mike, our one guy, like all men, had to have LUNCH. We girls usually grabbed a banana and kept on riding. No. Lunch was necessary, so we made him cook, often wonderful cheese omelets. Sometimes he cooked dinner as well. He was a good cook and enjoyed it. When my husband Max was out of town we often settled for "supper:" a couple of beers and some hunks of cheese. Fond memories and now new fond memories . . . .

These days, Shelly's the organizer. Like her mother, my good friend Joan, world-class horsewoman, Shelly gets it done; she organizes a three-day clinic at her farm and the others empty their barns to support it. It's nice to hand over the reins, the reign if you will, to Shelly. She decides on the dates, sends me my plane ticket, picks me up at the airport, offers me "supper" when we get home, our traditional beer and cheese, and when it's all over, she drives me back to the airport. Seattle is Microsoft country where luckily few have noticed that Wall Street has tanked and we are in a recession, so life goes on almost as usual. Shelly runs a first-rate business; her riders' basics are sound and the horses are lovely. They can afford to buy the best, and Shelly has a good eye. The whole program is excellent. She does it all my way, much better than I could, as do my other "Seattle children."

Tammy, the loose-horse super talent, always brings a bunch of "skins" she rides herself and a batch of students as well. Under my wing in the '70's, Tammy was called back fifth for the afternoon ride-off in the coveted Maclay Finals in Madison Square Garden, went back to the hotel to take a nap, overslept, and missed the course walk. Meanwhile, I am sprouting grey hairs, screaming at her father to find her, which he finally did. She learned the course in a heartbeat and stayed fifth. She could have won if she had put more into it, but that is Tammy: enormous talent, but not much program. She attracts students like herself, and they all ride well, but are not interested in the fine points. Her outfit is rather like a pirate ship. They blow into town, looking haphazard and disorganized, but before you know what's happened, they have won a couple of good classes—right under your nose, and they're off, clattering down the road. Tammy's way works for her, and that's what matters. My own outfit in the '70's often felt like a pirate ship, all helter-skelter: husband, two young boys, big, broken down farm, more business than I could handle, but . . . it was fun . . . .

Mike and Cathy eventually married and have wonderful, talented children, Sean and Lauren, now in their 20's, who train with my friend and colleague, world-class rider, Norman Dello Joio. Their kids sometimes stay over at the farm during the summer, but now we have progressed beyond cots and sleeping bags. Unspoiled and unentitled, they are as hard-working as their parents and often help me, schooling horses and teaching students.

On the fringes and somewhat faded, I usually do three groups of seven or eight riders at a clinic. In Seattle they empty their barns, so sometimes I do five groups—ten hours of teaching each day—Friday, Saturday, Sunday—plus helping them in between with assorted green and/or problem horses.

The fifth member of the group, Shaina, lives in the East now and called us one evening "to kill five birds with one stone" as she put it, the four "children" and me the semi-retired den mother. We agree we like having fun making money, mixing our avocation and our vocation. We still do some coast-to-coast business. Shelly has leased my horse, Mikey, to a client, and my clinic out there is profitable for all of us.

Our shared passion, the horses, has evolved into an understanding and trust like no other. Those long-ago summers of early mornings and late nights of hard work, feeding, caring for, and training our beloved horses remains with us all today. Together we've had trips to the winner's circle at the horse shows, trips home empty-handed, and even a few trips to the hospital. The good always outweighs the bad even if there is a stretch of bad. We are all glad to continue and improve our skills by learning from each other.

When they pour me on the airplane Sunday night, the red-eye to New York, I am sleepless with exhaustion and pride and delight that they are carrying the torch forward into the new century. It all works well probably because there are three thousand miles between us. The beauty of a clinic is that I am here today, gone tomorrow. They take what works and incorporate it into their system. They toss what doesn't work. I'm gone to manage my own crumbling empire and leave them to manage theirs. Most of all I am grateful for my "leg up" from them and proud of them for doing it my way but much better each in his or her own individual style.

IV.

Minutiae On and Off the Farm

Nail Polish

The mother of two grown boys and now grandmother of two little girls, I enlisted the aid of the six-year-old daughter of a friend when I went shopping at The Red Pony, a delightful, little-girl gift shop at the horse show. I figured Sarah could help me choose cute, little matching outfits for my girls. Wrong. Not a tomboy, but into REAL girlie things, she quickly picked up a little plastic case in which were several bottles of various shades of clear nail polish tinted red, green, blue and yellow.

"Look, look, look," Sarah exclaimed, her adorable Irish brogue lengthening the "ooo's," turned the case one way and the other. "There are stars and sparkles too." She couldn't think about anything else in the store but the nail polish. I, on the other hand, had not given nail polish a thought since I was ten years old . . . when my grandmother died. Suddenly her Irish voice came back to me, echoing down the years.

"Clear nail polish for grandmothers and little girls. Red nail polish for grown up ladies like Mary." Mary Leahy, a friend of my mother's, had THE most beautiful nails; long, perfectly shaped, shiny and red. Revlon's Fire and Ice. I even remembered the name of the color. (Sarah's mother's maiden name is also Mary Leahy)

Looking closely at the little bottles, I decided my Nana would have approved. The nail polish was clear, just slightly tinted, the stars and sparkles were a twenty-first-century improvement, so we bought three cases, one for Sarah and one for each of my granddaughters.

I had been anxiously wondering how I would entertain Sarah in the bleachers all afternoon while the horse show was in progress. Now, I knew. We could do our nails to while away a sunny afternoon at the horse show, just as years ago my Nana and I whiled away rainy afternoons on the farm. Best of all was the promise of whiling away quiet afternoons with Maxine and Margot . . . doing our nails.

Tiny Triumphs

The Madoff winter of 2009 was long and harsh, weather wise and otherwise. The sky is falling on Wall Street and everywhere else, but here at Coker Farm we have been living in our little bubble and entertaining ourselves with tiny triumphs which brighten our days.

One lease horse, Stevie, came home to roost; his rider's father lost his job. In an effort to save money the lessees had cut back on training and lessons, so the horse returned to us rather mixed up. In January Stevie came back well-fed, sleek and sound, but his brain was fried, and right away I knew I had a winter project. To regain his courage and confidence, he would need a lot of slow work.

The first day I rode him in the indoor ring he was tense and nervous, ears twitching, chomping on the bit, trying to go fast and sideways. He was a homebred, raised here on the farm, and had been an easy, brave, uncomplicated colt. "Will he regain his equanimity?" was the question I asked myself, slowing him to a walk and petting him on the neck to reassure him. All winter long we made the effort to get the tack on him every day even if it was a cold, short ride, as was often the case. After several weeks he was able to trot calmly around the ring but he was still pretty fiery at the canter, so I mixed short canters with long, slow trots. As the canter improved, I introduced some random rails on the ground in preparation for jumping exercises. No dice. He was terrified and would not go near the rails. In my salad days I'd have given him a smack and spurred him on, but with his routine of bucking and balking, he had been trying to get me hurt all winter, so I wisely dismounted and led him, first over the rails and finally over low jumps. A month went by, and he was finally brave enough to follow another horse over low jumps and ultimately jump a few easy ones on his own. Every day he is getting more relaxed and braver; even outdoors and through the woods when we got a break in the weather he gamely hops over little logs and wood piles.

When the real riders get home from Florida in April, he will be ready to be kicked around over more challenging jumps. Proof of his progress is that his little, twittering ADHD ears are mostly pointing forward as he focuses on the job at hand and where he is going instead of nervously checking out the rider and all his surroundings. Recently he bravely followed my granddaughter's reliable pony, Misty, over all the little jumps in the outdoor ring and then went on to jump them alone. My friend up North, Shaina, thought she could sell him come spring. I was not that optimistic, but a lease/sale would be nice or even a summer lease would do. He's a nice horse, and indeed someone did want him. Shaina sold him for me.

Another tiny triumph this winter has been little Eliza, nine-year-old daughter of my good friend, Moira. Last winter they found a wonderful pony in Florida, but when they got it home to Millbrook, it proved to be not so wonderful. In the cold, windy weather and in the absence of training and supervision, the pony soon became too frisky and frightened the child. It is so easy to make mistakes in our game, it's a wonder we ever dare to buy any equines at all. The best pony in the world needs some structure and supervision, even if it's just a chase around the longe line. Our pony, Frosty Lad, was the exception that proved the rule; all we ever did is saddle him up and throw my frightened son Philip on board. Frosty did the rest, and his memory lives on. Now Phil is in his forties and fearlessly jumping huge fences at the horse shows.

When Eliza started coming this winter, she mostly walked and trotted my granddaughter's pony, Misty, with a few short canters. While her mother took lessons, I would make a couple of very low cross rails, 4"-6" high to tempt her. Soon we noticed she was carefully and slowly trotting Misty over them. Then one day I gave her a little pattern of three cross rails to do, trotting or cantering whichever she preferred. A few more weeks went by and soon she was cantering, not just three jumps but a half a dozen. Gradually the little jumps grew; and Eliza could do a course of eight 2' fences at the canter, no problem. A year later she and Misty were winning classes at competitive horse shows.

Now she is relaxed and unafraid, Eliza shows us that genes count for something; she has her mother Moira's good instincts and she "sees the jumps," as we say. That means that when she canters toward the jump, she knows where she is and, not so surprisingly, knows when and where her pony will leave the ground and jump. In all fairness we have to give Misty some credit for finding the jumps; her good rhythm and balance and pace make it easy.

Likewise Moira's big, grey Sam, by the famous world-class Irish jumper, Cruising, who once won the World Cup, "finds the jumps," and he has gotten better at it over the years, for Moira has that great knack for staying out of his way and letting him jump the jumps. Many riders find that very hard; as they approach the jump, it is "go. No, don't go. No, GO!"

Moira and Sam's partnership has been improving exponentially all winter long as we make increasingly difficult patterns of fences for them to negotiate. We change the jump course a couple of times a week to keep us all from getting bored. This pair has proved to be great entertainment, for so far there is nothing they cannot do. Here again we have tiny triumphs; it is one thing to do hard patterns at home in our own familiar ring and quite another to do them at a horse show where there are lots of distractions. Many of us can be world-class riders at home. We joke that Moira and Sam could win one of the National Equitation Finals, but luckily we'll never have to prove it as Moira is well over eighteen, the age limit. Besides, Sam is quirky and easily distracted, so a good performance in an alien ring is unlikely for him, but come spring, we will ask him that question. Mind you now, this horse still will not let you ride him back and forth to the indoor ring in a high wind, so we know to proceed carefully at his first few shows. Meanwhile, we have lots of fun challenging him and bragging.

A new pony, Casablanca, stayed with us when our tenant moved out. He also has lovely, natural balance and easily does all the little jumping exercises I present to his good-riding owner, Sam. Keen, dedicated, and talented, Sam will have a bright future if we show him the way and "stay out of his way," as a great horseman once said. Short on basics, he couldn't tell what diagonal he was on at the trot unless he looked over the pony's shoulder. By feeling and listening, he figured out that enigma in a couple of days. There's lots to work on, and lots to work with. I'm looking forward to a series of tiny triumphs for him all winter long. I'm delighted he is here.

A brand new candidate for tiny triumphs this winter is Farnley Bit of Blue. Like my new rider Sam, there's lots to work on and lots to work with. An unbroken, five-year-old, medium pony who has simply been a companion for an old retired horse, Blue doesn't know about living in a stall, having spent his entire life in a field with a run-in shed. Wearing a saddle and bridle is a new experience for him as well. I've been leading him around the farm and in the indoor ring, so he gets an idea of what's out there. We've been leaning on his back, but so far no one has ridden him yet. We hoped it would all go well and indeed he is doing just that. In a year's time Blue was teaching youngsters to ride and indeed he is doing just that.

There's no better way for me to start a cold, winter day than a ride on my current pet, Blink. His calm, mild disposition makes him an ideal old lady's horse to ride cross country, but it doesn't help him to be an aggressive, competitive show jumper. For both reasons, he did not earn a ticket to Florida this year; though well able, he's not competitive enough to be a winner, and he is a lovely, safe conveyance for me. On mild days we enjoy the neighboring woods and fields and when the weather is severe, we find refuge in the spacious and inviting indoor ring. The only better way for me to start a winter day is to watch Debbie McCarthy—old friend, horsewoman and rider, jump Blink over challenging fences in the indoor ring. His courage, talent, and scope are always evident in these schools, and he even focuses well and cares enough to leave the jumps up. We've been jumping him once or twice a week, often enough to remind him he is a good jumper.

These are just a few of the tiny triumphs we've enjoyed here at Coker, even though the sky is falling everywhere else. There is always something interesting to do with the horses and people. Most improve in stages of tiny triumphs.

On Sleeping Outside

Lately I have been sleeping outside, an old habit left over from my teen years in Vermont. During the summer I only needed a blanket and a pillow as I stretched out on one of the *"liegestühle"* (chaise lounges.) The dogs sleep on the other one.

What is lovely about sleeping outside in the summer is the awesome stillness now that the peepers have shut down. There is no sound anywhere unless the wind rustles a few leaves. The only light in view is the one on the flag and flagpole in front of the barn erected in honor of a friend's nephew who died in the World Trade Center. Everywhere else there is only darkness and quiet. Even the road out front is still.

During the night the silence is occasionally broken. The coyotes sometimes yowl in the sandpit at the back of the farm. They are more apt to be vocal when the moon is full, so lately I've heard a lot from them. It always is an eerie sound, reminiscent of the wolves in Dr. Zhivago. Other nocturnal noises nearer at hand are the dogs snoring, snuffling and scratching, which happens randomly all night long. Occasional cars driving in and out are only momentary disturbances. One airplane always flies over from northwest to southeast at about 2 or 3 am. It is very high and I almost don't hear it.

Now that it is cooler, I sleep under our old sleeping bag that Max and I used on cold nights at the farm in Vermont when we were up there skiing. We used to sleep in front of the fireplace, for it took the house several days to thaw out after we turned the heat on. Luckily I have no sense of smell, having fallen with my horse over fifteen years ago, for surely the army-green bag with a plaid interior stinks. One of these days I'll get it dry cleaned, so the Board of Health doesn't arrest me.

My "bed" faces the east, so I can watch the moon rise and proceed across the sky from northeast to southwest. This week the moon is full, and the backyard is as bright as day. As the moon sets around 5 or 6 am, the stars are very bright, especially the Eastern star just over the big tree by the river.

Snuggled in my warm, narrow bed I wait for dawn to creep over the hill, as it always does. The stars slowly fade, the last being the Eastern star by now lost beyond the branches of the big, old tree. Traffic on the road is picking up; commuters are already rushing to their jobs, the sound of their fast cars echoing off the cliff on the other side of the road. Meanwhile three cars have left the property, "significant others" who live here or random poachers off to jobs elsewhere. Incoming cars include the muckers' noisy, muffler-impaired vehicle as they come here to clean out stalls. Soon lights are on all over the farm, even the indoor ring, like a giant ocean liner, where Ramon, who is in charge of maintenance, is dragging the dirt to make sure the footing is perfect for our horses. "No foot, no horse" is an old adage and true. Ground that is too deep or too hard sooner or later lames up the toughest horse.

Westchester Airport opens at 6 am, so soon thereafter the sky is full of planes crossing overhead. All I hear is distant drones, for they climb quickly to their intended altitudes. Sometimes I can hear the far away whistle of trains in Katonah, Bedford Hills, or Mt. Kisco urging commuters to grab their coffee and newspaper and make a run for it.

Homer's rosy-fingered dawn arouses the birds, and they chirp merrily as they pick through their breakfast at the birdfeeder. A couple of angry crows sometimes caw at me, for I am not, in their eyes, a regular.

Soon, John Donne's "busy old fool, unruly sun" peeps over the hill, and it is time for me to get up. There's frost everywhere today; meadows and fence lines are shimmering in the early morning sunlight. Even my sleeping bag is sparkling though it kept me toasty warm, and I can see my breath in the clear, morning air. My nights of sleeping outside are numbered. Soon winter will be upon us, but this place is "a still point in a turning world."

Multiple Miracles: Popcorn Pups

We bred our Jack Russell, Miracle to my sister's Jack, Scout About, over Labor Day weekend, and to quote my son Philip, by the middle of October she "looked ready to pop." Amazed at the short gestation period for canines, he exclaimed, "She's like a microwave oven. Put in the kernels and when the bell rings, out pops the popcorn."

And so it seemed, for the pups were born Monday night, October 20, not without drama. In the late afternoon I came back from the barn to the house with the dogs, and suddenly Miracle vanished. Even though I knew darn well dogs about to whelp want to disappear and do it all on their own, I somehow managed to let Miracle slip away. With the other three dogs as the deputies, I searched the farm and up and down the road, calling and calling. Darkness was falling fast, and so was the temperature. Having the pups somewhere outdoors was not a good plan. Besides, this was her first litter, and considering her a bit of a flibbertigibbet, I was not at all sure she would be a good mother.

Miracle herself was rather a miracle. Her father's sperm languished frozen in a sperm bank for ten years before being mated with Sister, Miracle's mother. Miracle also survived being hit by a car out on the road. She broke her neck in five places. The vet declared he never got to do this operation, for the dog was already dead. Not Miracle, so I should not have doubted that she would pull off yet another miracle.

Finally at 10 pm, I gave up searching for her and bedded down in my sleeping bag on the lawn in hopes she would come back during the night. There was no moon. Suddenly the dark stillness was broken by muffled, angry growling coming from underneath our garden shed. Sure that it was Miracle, for her mother Sister was asleep next to me, we roused ourselves and went to have a look. Lying on my belly, I reached in, calling her soothingly. No dice. She kept on growling, and I knew if I grabbed

Miracle and her Pups.

her by the collar, she'd bite me. Armed with a flashlight and thick gloves, I tried again. This time I managed to drag her out snarling and settled her comfortably in the downstairs bathroom.

Several hours later the pups started slowly arriving. Miracle proved to be a good mother licking them dry one by one and then nursing them. The ultrasound said there were eight pups, and after six were born, an hour went by, and I worried that perhaps the missing two had been born under the shed before I pulled Miracle out. I grabbed the flashlight and crawled under the shed as far as I could and shone the flashlight around. No pups there, T.G., and while I was gone searching, Miracle gave birth to the last two to my surprise and joy. She produced four black-and-tans, three black-and-whites, and one brown-and-white for me; I named him Popcorn. There were eight little miracles, ten actually considering Miracle's own birth and her broken neck.

The Mouse and Nurse Diesel

All summer long when I opened the cabinet door next to the kitchen sink where we keep the tub of dry kibble dog food, there would be a frantic scratching noise. Every day a hungry mouse, possibly the same mouse, would struggle to escape up the slippery sides of the tall, plastic barrel. Before doling out the dog food, I would have to carry the tub out to the deck and tip it on its side, so the mouse could skitter out and escape. It became a daily ritual that came up as a topic of conversation with "Nurse Diesel," the soul of kindness but a bear about cleanliness and a passionate enemy of varmints, rodents, and all purveyors of dirt and germs.

The subject arose because Max's hospice room opened out into a lovely garden. Soft summer air and a full moon impelled us to leave the doors wide open all night.

Nurse Diesel was quick to scold us. "You have to close the doors after dark. Otherwise all kinds of varmints come in."

"What sort of varmints?" I asked.

"Well, mostly mice," she admitted, and I told her about our greedy mouse, (or mice?) at home.

She was quite horrified and lectured me about the many diseases they carry.

Not wanting to argue that I had always lived in old houses often frequented by harmless, apparently clean-enough mice, I took another tack and said,

"It's such a beautiful evening. Look at the moon. It's full."

"Okay," she replied, "but be sure you keep the door to the hall closed."

"Oh, I will," I assured her and promised to chase out any rodents that dared to enter.

The next morning when she appeared with breakfast, she had a suggestion.

"You know, I was thinking about your mouse. Why don't you put a little dish of kibble next to the big bin? Then he won't get stuck in it."

I suppressed a smile and did as she advised. Now our mice dine every night stress and danger free, thanks to Nurse Diesel, and in fairness I should admit she is right; some varmints are indeed carriers of terrible diseases.

Vermont Mice

If you don't like mice, don't even think of visiting our little, red, eighteenth-century farmhouse in Vermont. It sits on a mountain top, the views are breathtaking, but the mice police the place and consider it their own. We are just the occasional visitors who pay the taxes.

The first thing you notice when you walk into the kitchen would be the ubiquitous mouse turds even if I remember to leave the electronic, alleged "mouse-chaser" plugged in. The Vermont Country Store swears by the contraption, but I have my doubts. Cleaning up the little, dry, black turds is not that hard.

Any visitor to the farm is at the mercy of the previous one when it comes to mouse patrol. For example, I forgot to turn upside down the kitchen waste basket last time, and luckily for the mouse, my good friend Babs stopped by a few days later, and sure enough, a hungry, frantic mouse greeted her from the bottom of the trash can. She scolded him roundly as she rescued him, "If you have nine lives like most cats, you only have eight left. You'd better be careful." She set him free outside, and the moral of that anecdote is to turn aside or upside down all waste baskets, or there will be an epidemic of starved mice. (No way for any of us to begin a relaxing holiday.)

The other axiom for departing visitors is to make sure both toilet lids are down or, you guessed it, expect to find drowned mice next time. Someone figured out a handful of mothballs in each bed saves sweeping out mouse turds and sometimes mouse nests before unrolling your sleeping bag. These are just the few parameters that make life easier, and possibly cleaner, if you think wild, Vermont, country mice are dirty.

The mice may not be dirty, but they can be noisy, running up and down in the walls throughout the night. My solution is to shout and bang my bedroom slipper on the wall. That usually quiets them down for a few hours at least.

Needless to say, leaving delicacies, or for that matter anything edible, out on the counter or the table in Vermont is considered an open invitation to the feast. Mice are not bashful about helping themselves to whatever they can find to eat. By all means, keep the cheese in the refrigerator and everything else secure in chew-proof containers like the microwave and refrigerator. In Vermont we have a cabinet behind the old, black, wood stove that is lined with tin and impervious to mice; it is safe to leave everything there. It would not be wise to leave a little dish of kibble out like we do in New York. In the dead of winter, food is so scarce in Vermont mice would travel from all over the state. In Westchester County food is plentiful year round as are rodent exterminators. Even our few, yet to be exterminated, barn mice can't be bothered to help themselves to our paltry cup of kibble in the kitchen a hundred yards away.

Ironically, the alleged "dirty mice" actually work for me sometimes. There have been over the years anal visitors who vehemently vacuumed the house from top to bottom, even the window sills full of dead flies. No need to call a cleaning service, or worse yet, clean the place myself.

When I have to be gone months at a time "down county" with the "flatlanders," back in Westchester, it is comforting to know on cold, winter nights or hot, summer days, that the mice are looking after the place for me, and aside from some mouse turds here and there, there is no real damage or disease at all. There are no diseases within miles for them to carry around and after all they are not rats . . . .

My New Thermos

Fellow student Hank's retro '70's coffee thermos caught my eye the first day our writing class met, but it did not catch my brain until the next week when I was in the hardware store shopping for duct tape. (We go through a lot of duct tape, for you can't run a farm without a lot of duct tape and baling twine). I noticed an extensive, and probably expensive, array of thermoses, all shapes and sizes.

"Hmmm," I thought. "I should get a thermos for soup to take to Max in the hospital." Hospital food is bland at best; I noticed Max was not eating much. Even when suffering from viral meningitis, his good nature prevailed, and he did not complain about the food. "Remember," I told myself, "this man has survived over forty-five years of your cooking, not to mention, no food at all in Germany during World War II when he was a child." I do not remember his ever complaining about the meals I prepared. Admittedly my discovery early on of the little timer on the stove was a real breakthrough. Raw, over-cooked, or worse yet, burned dinners became less frequent and finally disappeared altogether. Mind you, I still avoid vague recipes that say, "cook until done."

Anyway, in the hardware store, I selected a squat, fat, wide-mouthed thermos, perfect for soups. Since Max retired, lunch had become a fixture, a pleasant pause in the day, instead of a banana on the fly from the barn to the ring. Max especially liked homemade soup, and luckily, I discovered *Progresso* soups, well-named I must say. Our favorites, heated right out of the can, were Lentil, Beef Barley, Chicken and Wild Rice; anything really, they are all good.

Now thanks to the new thermos there was a new ritual: hot soup every day in the hospital. This thermos is allegedly unbreakable, and so it seems to be, having survived a long winter of bumps and falls. My little, red thermos of the '70's, on the other hand, had to have several new innards inserted, for the slightest knock would shatter its glass which was fortunately easily and cheaply replaced.

Winter is gone, and so is Max, but the first day of class there was Hank and his retro '70's coffee thermos, reminding me of my long gone easily broken red thermos I used all winter in the '70's when I was renting stalls at an indoor ring in lower Westchester. Without my trusty thermos of hot coffee, I would not have survived those long cold afternoons teaching in that dank, dark indoor ring.

In the '70's before we had our own luxurious indoor ring we had to rent stalls somewhere, usually in lower Westchester: Boulder Brook or Secor or Kenilworth for a few months when it was too awful to ride outside. Every afternoon I'd pile the kids and their tricycles, my coffee thermos and their Cheerios into the Volkswagen for the trek to the indoor ring. Luckily both of them inherited their father's good disposition and cheerfully rode their tricycles, and later bicycles, and munched on Cheerios while I taught my students and drank my coffee. We seldom got home before 7pm, but the Cheerios and coffee kept us going 'til suppertime.

Now thanks to Hank there is a new ritual on Thursdays when our writing class meets. Instead of 21st century Starbucks frappacino grabbed on my way to class, I indulge myself with a real thermos of real coffee. To disprove the extent of this indulgence, I must admit that most days I just heat water in the microwave and pour in the instant coffee and milk. As winter approaches I suspect I may develop the habit of freshly brewed coffee every day with the balance of the pot going in the thermos with me to the barn. Freshly brewed coffee is the best, and coffee from a thermos has an unmistakable flavor of its own.

Thanks, Hank, for reminding me about one of life's little luxuries.

My New Lawnmower

All winter long while we were concentrating on jumping clear rounds at the horse shows in West Palm Beach, the grass in the backyard of my turnkey condo has been quietly growing. Finally as it was nearly knee-high, I noticed that the place looked a bit shaggy and added "lawnmower" to my Home Depot list of little amenities the condo needed.

At Home Depot, Jim, an ageless, big, black guy with a silver ring on his finger and a gold one through his nose, had just what I needed—or so he thought. I told him my backyard was tiny, 25' x 50'±, but he had grand ideas for me. He proudly pointed out a diesel mower that could cut the grass as high or as low as I liked. It cost only $200 and came in a little box considering its size, which only means some mechanical genius is needed to assemble it. That I am not, nor is there "staff" with or without extraordinary mechanical aptitude. Actually, there is no "staff" at all; I am it. Meanwhile, down the aisle I saw a cute, little, green Scotts hand mower.

"What about that one?"

"Oh, missus, you don't want that little one."

"Don't missus me" I thought and said, "I think that's just exactly what I want."

A $50 sale didn't look as good to him as a $200 sale, but he was a good sport, knowing that something was better than nothing. He searched in vain far up into the rafters: no little mower in a box.

"Well, just sell me that floor model," I said, thinking, "Such a deal. It's already assembled."

"Oh, missus, I can't do that."

"Call your supervisor. I really want that one." And so he did, and that supervisor called his supervisor, and an hour later, I was in the check-out line. The next glitch was that the check-out person had to call his supervisor to make sure it was okay to sell a floor model. It was, so I paid and Jim wheeled the mower out to the car for me. He loved my little, red VW convertible and hoisted the mower in saying,

"Missus, I was afraid we couldn't get it in your car, but with the top down it's easy."

He refused my tip and probably regaled his wife that night with a story about the silly, old lady who had to have a little floor-model hand lawnmower.

Little did he know I had spent my childhood with just such a mower. It was green, and, I think, also made by Scotts. The "lawn" at our farm in Vermont was so hilly that a hand lawnmower was the only safe mower for pre-teens to use, so that was it, and for years I mowed, and that lawn was no 25' x 50' patch of grass either.

As I unloaded the mower at home I had a sinking feeling the blades were not sharp enough to cut the tough south Florida grass, and ran my index finger gently along one of the blades. I accidentally drew blood and concluded the blades were indeed sharp enough, and so they were. I proved to be a disgrace to my breeding; my father worked for Johnson and Johnson for forty-four years, but I knew in my heart there was not a single Band-Air in the condo. There was, however, duct tape in the car which worked just fine.

In less than an hour our shaggy backyard was shaved and shorn, the long grass raked and dumped in the garbage can. An easy, satisfying job well-done, if I say so myself.

Learning Styles at the Horse Gym

Our new horse gym has provided good entertainment during an otherwise quiet winter. "Why a horse gym?" friends asked.

"Labor-saving," I answered, "And also safety."

It is labor-saving in that when horses come back after an injury or an illness, they need hours of walking and jogging every day for weeks before they are fit enough to gallop and jump. Trying to ride six properly last fall, two which were bound for Florida to horse show and the others in basic training, I felt I was just not doing enough for each of them. A half hour on the gym and a half hour under tack should bring about a better outcome: fit horses ready to do their job well.

The safety issue is one I cannot overlook. Young, fit horses and even old, broken horses can be rambunctious. I don't need to get bucked off. A half hour or more on the gym should take the edge off the wild ones and reduce the likelihood of my landing in the hospital.

Made in Germany, the horse gym is a knock-off of a human treadmill, but it is clearly designed for equines. Until it moves, the ramps on and off resemble a horse van; climbing up the back ramp, standing in a narrow stall, and climbing down the front ramp is an experience familiar to all show horses that do a lot of traveling. How clever of the designers to trade on what the horses already know.

The directions in the accompanying pamphlet are adamant and vague: "Introduce the gym slowly," but how is not really explained. First we laid in a supply of carrots. A new "expert" who writes horse how-to books for kids stubbornly declares feeding treats of any sort to horses is a very bad practice; you teach them to bite. I could not accomplish much without carrots and certainly they facilitated introductions to the horse gym. I believe treats distract anxious horses and reassure the genuinely frightened ones, but I'm old, old-fashioned, and what do I know? I know what works, and carrots work for me and for the horses.

We started by leading each horse on and off the gym, then stood him for several minutes on the mat, all the while offering him little bits of sliced carrots, for in the face of presumed danger, horses are comforted by treats. (We slice the carrots, thin-slice them actually, because carrots are expensive and we are stingy. We've found a little bit works as well as a half a carrot.) Also to take the edge off his fear at first, we gave each horse a little tranquilizer, 1cc of Acepromazine. For the more jittery ones we upped the dosage to 2 or 3 cc.

Not surprisingly, each horse reacted just about as we expected. The horse gym is installed in the shed adjoining the barn in the hopes that eventually we will be able to watch from the tack room and barn once the horses get used to walking on it.

All horses are super sensitive to visual changes in their environment, so it was no surprise that upon their first introduction every equine got tall, bug-eyed, and snorty as we led him into the shed.

"Now what is this contraption?" they each asked. Once reassured with a few bites of carrots, most were okay with individually walking on and off the gym.

Some horses, once we turned it on, took much longer than others to get used to the forward motion, at first set very slow. We started with the tamer, calmer candidates, so we could learn how fast we could proceed.

First on the gym was Blink, my current pet, an Argentinean *Selle Francais* (French-bred in Argentina) beloved by all for his easy-going, calm temperament. After a couple of snorts at the new machine, he climbed amiably aboard. The moving belt under him did not alarm him; he just calmly put one foot in front of the other, and within a couple of days, we omitted the tranquilizer and he's been marching along like a trouper ever since. He doesn't need attendants or carrots anymore, but we give him a carrot now and then anyway for good behavior.

Some of the others were not so easy and accommodating. The worst of the group, not surprisingly, was Firefly, who should have been named Firecracker. He has been laid up for two years with a tendon injury and now is "ready to go back to work," according to the vet. Even tranquilized, he is a pistol, so I am glad to start him on the gym, easier said than done. After several weeks of being coaxed with carrots and at first heavily sedated, he has finally succumbed to walking calmly to nowhere or let's hope to a brilliant career in show jumping. We are extra careful not to startle him, and so far, he is okay with the horse gym, but not yet able to handle it alone. Someone has to be by his side doling out carrots as needed.

It has been a learning experience for all of us to introduce our horses to this marvel of engineering. We hope the gym will help us be better prepared for the upcoming horse shows, and fit for life in general.

The Pulley Rein

Last week one of our nice ladies got run off with across an open field out back. Helplessly screaming and digging her heels into her horse's sides, she only frightened him more, so he ran faster. Finally she bailed out. Clearly she did not know about the pulley rein, one of the five basic rein aids, and possibly the most important one to know. Horses, by nature creatures of flight, are much bigger and stronger than we are. It is important to know how to stop them.

To use the pulley rein, grasp the reins firmly in each hand, make a fist with your weaker hand, brace yourself stiff-armed by pressing down on the horse's neck just in front of his withers, and pull with all your might with your strong hand, arm, shoulder, and back. In an open field you can force your horse to circle as you slow him down. On a narrow path, you have to be careful not to run him into trees. The horse is more apt to take off in open spaces, and an alert rider should be able to catch him before he really gets going.

This was the second time in less than a month that our nice lady got run away with, and the first time was partly my fault. She was nearby when my colt leapt exuberantly over a rail on the ground instead of just cantering it. He startled her horse, and he was off across the field, running toward the barn, home, safety. She clung like a burr, but screaming, oblivious to our shouts to circle the horse. After she bailed out, I galloped over to make sure she was all right, mumbled something about the pulley rein, and rode off. The next time she was not so lucky; she broke her shoulder.

The most famous person I taught about the pulley rein was Sylvia Plath, the poet, in the late fifties. Before she was famous, I was a student in her English class at Smith College. Even then she was intimidating: brilliant, beautiful, strict with her hair pulled back in a schoolmarmish bun. She noticed my jeans and paddock boots (and probably the horsy aroma that surrounded me) and was smart enough in our one-on-one conference to put me at ease by talking about horses. Later she showed me a poem she was working on about her experience of being run away with, which she later published, "Whiteness I Remember." She vividly described the experience of helplessness "the world subdued to his run of it," with faint white shades of Moby Dick. Right away I told her about the pulley rein, offered to demonstrate it on my horse Coker, stabled at the college barn, and even encouraged her to come ride him and try out the pulley rein which she did one spring day.

She arrived at the barn, hair in a ponytail, dressed in jeans and sneakers. No hard hat in those days. I didn't wear one either. Today's safety mongers would have chased us from the premises.

In his meeting with her, Coker was affable and entertaining, bowing and shaking hands, turning his lip inside out, Mr. Ed style. (I did not tell her that just the week before Coker had cornered the blacksmith in his stall, and I had had to be summoned from class to rescue him. Coker did not like men, especially vets and blacksmiths). In any case, she was enchanted, I demonstrated the pulley rein, and she climbed on Coker herself and proved to all that she understood how to use it, saying: "if we cannot even control our horses, how can we control our lives."

Her analogy was appropriate; horses are people too and need to be handled properly. The pulley rein is a helpful tool, but brute force simply does not work, for horses are considerably stronger than we are. That women compete on horseback against men at all levels of the spot, including the Olympic Games, is proof enough that physical strength is not the main issue. Calm assertiveness is what gets it done, just like in life.

Calm assertiveness comes naturally to the weaker sex. I do think the pulley rein is instrumental in helping women assert themselves over their big strong horses. The smart women eventually figure out how to coax their horses to do what they want them to do. The control freaks are assertive to a fault; my son calls them wood chippers like the woman in the movie *Fargo*.

My own family was slow to learn about the pulley rein. My parents were "seat of the pants" riders, with little formal equestrian education, so it was not surprising except to them, that when I was seven, my pony bolted, and I fell off, breaking my arm. It healed, and sooner or later I learned about the pulley rein. However, I neglected to teach my son Hans about it, for he was big and strong from childhood on. However, when he was in his early teens, a horse we were trying on Long Island in hopes of buying it for him ran off with him zigzagging around a field full of cedar trees. Helplessly, I watched as Hans managed to stop him. Naturally we did not buy him, and soon thereafter Hans learned about the pulley rein.

Years later I taught his daughter, my granddaughter Maxine, about the pulley rein, not a moment too soon as she is getting very bold and could get run off with, though her pony is usually well-behaved. As we rode down the lane to the back fields, I carefully demonstrated the pulley rein, she practiced it at the walk first, then as we got to the open fields, the trot, and before long, at the canter. Finally at full gallop, she breathlessly shouted, "it works!" as she calmly circled his mount at the far end of the field. It does work.

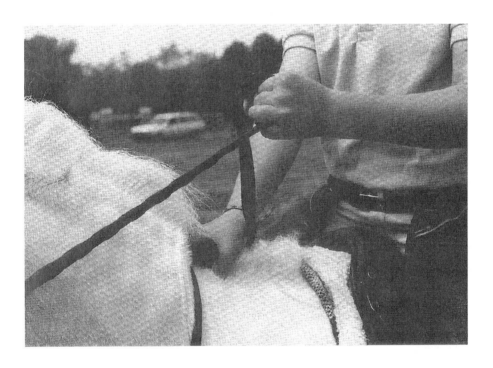

The Pulley Rein is demonstrated by
Cullen Latimer and Frosty Lad.

The Beaver Dam

All year long I have been watching our nearby neighbor's swamp fill up with water. Yes, we've had a lot of rain but not *that* much. Calls to the town of Bedford's wetlands commissioner were to no avail. All the trees were dying, but the local tree huggers did not care. Other neighbors who live right on the swamp complained that while they were out of town several trees in their backyard vanished. The stumps looked chewed, not sawed, and for the first time, even though the river is named Beaver Dam River, beavers were indeed the prime suspect.

The summer wore on, the water kept rising. Then there was a surface of green slime. Probably millions of mosquitoes were multiplying, but luckily no West Nile Disease, no malaria, no typhoid cases were reported. Finally one Sunday I took a hike all the way around the edge of the swamp. On the far side I found a giant beaver dam extending one hundred and fifty feet across the river and the swamp between two hillocks. It was so solid I could walk across it, so forget poking a few holes in it to let the water through. Chewed off tree stumps lined the banks on both sides.

In Vermont in the '50's, where we spent our summers, beavers were quite the nuisance. On the road to our farm there was a large pond where they moved in, built a big hut of a house, and dammed up the pond. It was all very cute until the water flooded the road. Then the local farmers took matters into their own hands; they shot the beavers and dynamited the dam, and that was the end of that problem until more beavers came back the next spring. Now the locals just dynamite the dam every couple of years, but they are not allowed to kill the beavers. Beavers are persistent; they simply rebuild.

When the water floods Route 121, and we need rowboats to get to town, maybe the town will do something. Dynamite would be too extreme; Manhattan would be flooded as the river feeds N.Y.C. reservoirs.

Our neighbor on the other side of the swamp, a spicy old lady, now in her nineties, is determined to "do something," whatever that means. When I showed her some pictures I took of the dam, she pointedly said:

"Well, what do we expect? The river is called the Beaver Dam River," and so it is on every map of Westchester County. Her son, a local contractor, is wisely consulting the authorities and trying to go through the right channels to solve the problem before she does.

Meanwhile the water is rising. It is only a couple of feet from flooding the road. Already our lower fields are under water. Luckily our barns and house are on high ground. We have been in contact with the authorities and received a copious memorandum from the New York State Department of Environmental Conservation Division Fish, Wildlife and Marine Resources regarding Permit Requirements Guidelines for Breech and Removal of Nuisance Beaver Dams. My neighbor's solution to tear down or dynamite the dam will not do.

My neighbor and I finally did take matters into our own hands. Since the water was rising and the town was stalling, the most appropriate and least expensive solution was offered by the American Humane Society who has promised to install six large pipes with screening on both ends of each pipe under the dam. Presumably then everyone will be happy. The swamp will be drained and go back to being a normal swamp, we hope. Some of the drowned trees will survive, the waters will recede from our lower fields, and the beavers can keep their dam intact. The cost, a mere $500 for the labor and $700 for the material provided by my neighbor's son who is in the construction business. My neighbor and I have agreed to split the cost which is nominal considering the effort and equipment involved. For a while, of course, nothing has happened, the beavers are building the dam higher every day, the waters are rising, and we are keeping our snorkels handy.

Epilogue: Last weekend the pipes were installed, the water is receding on all fronts, down six inches so far, Manhattan was not inundated; and we put our snorkels away . . . but the persistent beavers will not quit. They stopped-up the six big pipes under the dam and the water rose again. "Animal Control" installed six more pipes and so far we are enjoying our tiny triumph over the beavers and we hope we have solved the beaver problem for good, but I doubt it.

A Proposed Swarm

Thanks to an old connection, sparked by our devotion to a special horse, Dark Sonnet, I recently learned that a "swarm" is a family gathering and/or simply a group of friends and/or neighbors who work together doing a lot of odd jobs that just need doing. Busy as bees, they get the work done quickly and easily. It was a tradition practiced by the pioneers, building barns and such. Modern swarms are less ambitious, but helpful and necessary.

A farming friend and former student, Kathy, surfaced this spring, traveling all the way from her farm in Vermont with two daughters, her mother, and three equines. Arriving in her pickup and horse trailer with their own sleeping bags and towels, they stayed in my loft apartment; the horse and two ponies, with their own feed and bedding, in the barn. Kathy still rides well, thanks to her good start with Dark Sonnet, and her girls are as keen as she is. Kathy's mom was put to good use, taking notes and videos. When we were arranging for future lessons, I suggested Easter weekend as the kids were off from school.

"Oh, no," they chorused, "We can't do that. On Easter weekend we have our annual family swarm. We can't miss that."

For decades now they have been gathering at her family's thousand-acre dairy and vegetable farm in Saratoga to help her aging parents repair the ravages of winter. Years ago they swapped 20 acres of that lovely farm to an Olympic medalist for his special horse, "Dark Sonnet," for Kathy, a horse that launched her on a successful career of show jumping and cemented our lasting friendship.

When Kathy went off to college I bought Sonnet for my two sons for a song. By then he was old and lame but he did well for them too, for we only showed him occasionally. His greatest success was carrying my then working student, Andre Dignelli, to victory in the National Finals, held at the USET Training Center in Gladstone, N.J. Sonnet retired and Andre grew up to be one of the top horsemen in the country.

Since I too am an aging farmer of sorts, overwhelmed with a plethora of odd jobs, I decided to celebrate my birthday this year by inviting my family to a swarm at the Vermont farm. The guest/worker list includes Hans, my older son, now in his forties, his wife, Jennifer, my two granddaughters, Maxine, and Margot, as well as Philip, my younger son. The boys have done odd jobs with Dad all their lives, so the projects would be all too familiar. For decades, Max, my husband, quietly attended to these tasks whenever we were there on holiday, so I think of the farm as being turnkey, the only real maintenance being to mow the lawn and surrounding fields to keep the woods from encroaching. (Our neighbor, Mr. Potter, now in his eighties, has done "the mowin'" for decades. He is very modern, upscale, and dialed in; his tractor is equipped with air conditioner, oxygen and a satellite radio/TV/DVD.)

When I sat down to make a list for the swarm, I thought of at least fifteen jobs that needed doing, none of them urgent, but all of them necessary sooner or later. Now Max has been gone for several years, and the minor damages are multiplying. As usual, the snowplow wrecked some havoc; both the split rail fence and the stone wall need repair. Countless branches are scattered all over the yard; they should be gathered and put in boxes for kindling next winter. The old maple that fell several years ago is our main source of fire wood; more logs have to be split and stacked in the basement. A big birch limb came down last winter. It also needs to be cut for firewood. Lighter jobs include chopping away the suckers under the big pine tree and all the lilac bushes. Afterwards ashes from the fireplace must go under the lilacs. That is an old family tradition. My mother was adamant about how it was to be done. Leave some in the fireplace, so the fire will draw well. Do not fill the container to overflowing, so the ashes spill all over the floor when you carry them out. Make two or three trips if necessary, and spread them sparingly, not thickly. We could plant some hardy flowers in the big iron tub and along the stone walls. The hedge in front of the house needs trimming; we can hardly see over it out of the kitchen windows. There is plenty of work, but it should be fun too, and indirectly Max and Sonnet are responsible for our first swarm. May they rest in peace while we swarm.

"Is You Family?"

My friend, Emory Clark, recently returned from South Carolina, bringing news about Sarah, a ninety-year-old shriveled, shrunken, black woman who worked her entire life up until last year at his Milford plantation. Relieved of her lifelong duties of hoeing and raking, not to mention caring for the three Clark children, as well as her own ten, now grown, she lives in a spare, but to her swell, assisted living home in nearby Columbia.

"Ah eats and sleeps, winks and blinks," she reported to Emory who makes sure he visits her whenever he goes south. Every time he stops by, she always looks up at him proudly, saying:

"Ah *is* somebody."

On this particular day, Sarah was scheduled to go to the hospital across town for some tests, and she was anxious her visit with Emory would be cut short.

"Not at all," he assured her. I'll just ride back and forth with you."

In due time two beefy, rednecks, actually no-necks, according to Emory, arrived and hustled her into the ambulance. When the tall, blue-eyed, Emory announced he was coming with her, one of the no-necks looked up at him and asked summarily,

"Is you family?"

"Ah *is* family," Emory told him decisively, and so after a short pause he was permitted to ride in the ambulance back and forth to the hospital where fortunately her tests proved she was okay.

Later Emory mused on his declaration, "Ah *is* family" thinking, "these guys have no idea how very much we are family. No, we were not Jeffersons or Thurmonds, but her ancestors were slaves on the plantation before my great grandparents bought it. After they were freed, they refused to leave their Eden, which was home.

Now nearly one hundred and fifty years later, while a few have gone off to college (courtesy of Clark scholarships) and beyond, most of the black descendants are still there working while hunting and fishing in the swamp like their forebears, a provincial time warp. However, most are more computer literate than their boss, and they have chosen to live and die on the plantation.

When Emory took his leave from Sarah that evening, he already knew what she would say, tears in her big, brown eyes, "Thank you Emory. Ah appreciate it to the highest."

V.

Paintings, Prints, Portraits, Photos

Thomas Oldaker: Nineteenth Century Huntsman and Family Friend

For nearly five decades Thomas Oldaker has presided over my desk and for several decades before that, over my father's. He bought the old hunting print for a song in a pawnshop in Philadelphia in the bottom of the Depression when he was homeless and living on the couch in the Beta house at Penn.

"Homeless and buying pictures?" I queried. He answered, saying something about food for the soul, "like hyacinths," referring to the poem by James Terry White on that very subject, "Not By Bread Alone:"

> If thou of fortune be bereft
> And in the store there be but left
> Two loaves, sell one and with the dole
> Buy hyacinths to feed thy soul.

The caption on the picture declares that Thomas Oldaker, twenty years huntsman to the Berkeley Hounds in England, is mounted on his favorite Hunter, Brush. This print is a reproduction by Ketterlinus, Philadelphia, of the original engraving, published in 1810. I've never seen another copy although once I saw a portrait of Mr. Oldaker on his horse, Pickle. Pickle was apparently just a horse, not special like Brush.

Of the many hunting prints that surround us, this one has always been a family favorite. Thomas Oldaker is seated comfortably on Brush, about to blow his horn to summon from the woods behind the struggler hounds that do not yet surround him. Despite his twenty years of service as huntsman, he is still a healthy vigorous young-looking man. He is wearing a drab, brown long coat reaching over his knees, not the traditional "pink" coat and white breeches. Probably it is still cubbing season early in the fall when formal attire is not yet worn. Another hint that it is cubbing season is the bitch (female hound) standing in front of Thomas whose hanging dugs tell us that her pups were just recently weaned. Nine other hounds, each an individual different from the others, gather enthusiastically around their master.

Brush is not a beautiful horse, but very handsome, "a horseman's horse." He stands squarely on all four legs and gazes calmly into the distance as his rider summons the hounds. Not an ounce of fat on him anywhere, the horse like Thomas is all rippling muscle, "fit as a racehorse," as the saying goes. Even though he is dark brown and nondescript looking, a true horseman would notice him instantly for his wise calm eyes, his bony head, and his exceptionally athletic body. His dark coat gleams in the morning light. His nineteenth-century bobbed tail is perfectly trimmed. (Luckily the practice of bobbing tails has been banned as cruel, which it is)

This is a well-traveled print, accompanying first my father and then me, as we journey through our lives. It went with him from Philadelphia to Kansas City where he was a shipping clerk for Johnson and Johnson. Promoted to be New England Regional supervisor, he took Thomas Oldaker along and proudly hung him in his (first) office. From there they proceeded to Raritan, New Jersey, to found and run Ortho, the newly-formed pharmaceutical corporation. When my Dad, now known as "Big Phil," moved on to the headquarters in New Brunswick, N.J, Thomas Oldaker was looking a bit shabby and forlorn, so my father retired him to the likewise dilapidated old farm in Vermont where he presided over our dinner table until I hijacked him and took him along to college with me where he hung over my desk. Next he followed me and my husband Max to our first home in Manhattan, then on to a succession of garage apartments and our first house of our own. Some years ago I gave Thomas a face lift, had the print reframed, and now he is good to go for another century.

If I had to find a reason why this painting has been a family favorite for the better part of a century, I would have to say it is the diffused golden light that pervades the scene. The woods and fields behind feel distant and vague, as though painted with watercolor in contrast to the boldly drawn creatures in the foreground. Overall, the muted morning sunlight suffuses that world. In cubbing season, late August and most of September, hounds go out early, long before Homer's "rose-fingered dawn" and by mid-morning it is time to "call it a day" and head for home. And what a lovely golden day, not radiant but muted, the best light for sport in the field and elsewhere.

"Thomas Oldaker," twenty-six years Huntsman to the
Berkley Hounds, sitting on his favorite Hunter, Brush.
A Reproduction by Ketherlinus, Philadelphia, of the original
engraving, published in 1810. Engraved by R. Woodman.

"Ex Libris": More Keepers

A favorite print is "Ex Libris" because it could depict a whimsical event in my own library. In the center of the darkened scene is a pile of old books casually leaning against one another. A wily old fox has just run from left to right across the top of the books and is jumping, tail in the air, to safety—or to be snatched by the hounds in hot pursuit. One hound is poised precariously on the book ready to leap and grab his prey. Four others are nosing their way between the fallen books as they enthusiastically join the chase. Behind the books on the left is the huntsman, horn in hand, dressed in the traditional pink coat, white stock tie, and black cap. His high-headed gray steed is eagerly looking across the tops of the books, surprised no doubt to find himself in someone's library. Foxhunters and hounds will go anywhere in their pursuit of the fox, and the fox himself will try anything—henhouses, pig sties, cattle yards, libraries—anything to throw his enemies off the trail.

Clearly this is a foxhunter's dream, perhaps after he's spent a long day riding to hounds. Or maybe he fell asleep reading Gordon Grand's poignant tales of hunting in Millbrook or Anthony Trollope's *Hunting Sketches*, sportive portraits of foxhunters in the 19th century. In any case, only a true-blue bookish foxhunter could enjoy such a dream.

In the fifties my mother met the artist, Michael Lyne, out foxhunting (where else?) with our local pack, the Essex, in New Jersey. Sitting comfortably on his borrowed horse, he looked totally the Englishman, tall and lanky, already sporting a bushy moustache and spectacles under his top hat. No safe hunt cap for him, he was all about style. Young and not yet famous, he was touring America which to him meant fox hunting. He spent that winter living from hand to mouth, and he also managed to get a few commissions.

Ex Libris by Michael Lyne, 1955.

I remember he told us "Ex Libris" was his favorite painting. He did it when he was in his early twenties just a few years before we met him and enthusiastically described it to us. Years later I found it in a shop at the Devon Horse Show and grabbed it for a mere thirty-five dollars. It is now priceless, but not for sale.

A Family of Fox Hunters

Before he became famous, the British sporting artist Michael Lyne, painted a lovely portrait of my family when my sister and I were teenagers. My mother, secretary of the Essex Fox Hounds in Peapack, New Jersey, met him (where else?) out hunting. An engaging young man in his late twenties, he was "touring America," i.e., fox hunting with every pack of hounds in the country where he could beg, borrow or steal a horse to "ride to hounds" as well as bed and board in between hunting. My mother, always attracted to oddball waifs, cottoned to him and invited him to stay with us and hunt one of our horses. Hounds went out three days a week, so there was plenty of time for painting and conversation.

For a few dollars and some '50's hospitality my sister and I now have a priceless heirloom. Michael, already "frightfully British," stayed with us several weeks and had plenty of opportunity to observe us riding our favorite horses. Of course, we had to be riding our favorites for the portrait. What he captured best was the stance of the horses and the way the riders sat on them. His work was both impressionistic and accurate.

It was a fall day, probably November, and the hunt meet was at our farm, in the front field where only a corner of our dilapidated 18th century farmhouse peeked out from the left hind corner of the picture. Also in the background were the other hunt members and hounds vaguely drawn in. Overhead the gray-blue clouds hovered but did not threaten rain. A few leaves remained on the trees, but not many. In the distance were lovely blue hills, unmarred then by interstate highways and condominiums.

Gathered in the foreground were the four of us: father, mother, and two daughters. On the right were "Big Phil" and Mr. George; tall, stiff and imposing. Big Phil was decked out in his hunting pinks, and George was gleaming from his white stockings to his tall ears. Next to him, I was on my precious Kerry Spades, a dear but useless creature my parents bought for me as a three-year-old. She was an OK horse, and I loved her at the time, but in retrospect, I see she was virtually useless to me, too green and always getting hurt. She wasn't bad; she was just unlucky and untalented. Eventually we gave up on her, bred her, and raised a couple more no-talents . . . . What were we thinking. Clearly, we weren't.

Next to me was my sister Carol. Now she could "horseback" from an early age, and her horse, The Kitten, was larger than life. Though actually physically quite small, she excelled in every division at the horse shows; hunter, jumper, equitation, and she won all the point to points, Pony Club Rallies, and every other event offered to young kids and their horses. Michael Lyne really caught the ease and grace my sister has on a horse even today many years later.

Last but not least, is my mother on her Lady Ardmore, a hot Thoroughbred mare by Wizard's Play by Fair Play, sire of Man O'War. Bred in the purple, Lady fell on hard times. She ended up at the Empire Race Track somewhere in one of the New York boroughs, and my parents bought her for $100. She proved to be a good buy, even with all her quirks and her hot disposition. She had talent, and she could jump big jumps. It took my sister Carol and me almost a decade to learn how to ride her, but she is the one who definitely leapfrogged us into the big time. Every rider knows you are only as good as your horse. She was real good, and she made us look good. Meanwhile, our mother fox hunted her two or three days a week. She was a busy mare winning at horse shows; hunt meets, Pony Club Rallies, and other events besides carrying our mother over field and stream, fences of all sorts, as they fox hunted to the end of the day. Anyway, Michael Lyne's portrait of Mother on Lady is the most true-to-life portrayal of anyone on any horse that I have ever seen.

No portrait is perfect, and what Michael missed was how the horses' sizes as related to each other. Kitten was at least a foot smaller than Mr. George, but in the picture they look just a few inches apart. For years afterward my Mother scolded herself for not showing him a picture of the four of us next to each other. But it really did not matter. Michael did not realize how big my Dad was. Big Phil dwarfed Mr. George who was a huge 17.2 hands high. He is decked out in his hunting pinks and the direct gaze is definitely his. On the other hand, Carol's Kitten was indeed larger than life. There was nothing she could not do. She easily won everywhere. No wonder Michael Lyne thought she was 16.2 not 15.0 hands high. She thought so too.

A Family of Fox Hunters, 1960, by Michael Lyne.
Father Philip, the Author, Mother Mary, Sister Carol.

Decades after his visit to us in New Jersey, he became famous, and his early painting of "A Family of Fox Hunters," is unknown to the sporting arts aficionados, but we treasure the painting and those long ago days, the '50's and we will never sell our priceless painting.

A Treasured Painting

When I graduated from college, my parents gave me this painting of my favorite horse, Mr. Coker, by my favorite artist, C.W. Anderson. I appreciated it as much now as I did on that day long ago in June 1961. They were wise to give me a note explaining the gift, for they thought the process would be as much fun as the product, as indeed it was.

By the sixties, C.W. Anderson had become quite the renowned equine artist, commissioned by the rich and famous. Remembering who some of his earliest admirers were, he agreed to do a pastel for us. We knew Coker with his non-descript Canadian breeding and his head shaped like an ironing board was not exactly CW's type; he preferred the lovely Thoroughbreds, particularly the beautiful bays related to Man O'War. Coker was definitely not bred in the purple nor did he have a pleasant expression or disposition. At least he was the right color, bay.

The appointed day arrived, and the artist came to our farm to get to know Coker. CW's habit was to spend some quality time alone with his subject, usually sitting on his stool in the corner of the stall and occasionally sketching his impressions. I warned him that might not work for Coker who disliked men in general and really hated having humans of any sex loitering in his stall. His home was definitely his castle. We compromised by placing the stool at the door. Within a few minutes Coker chased him away, pencils and paper flying. The artist retreated reluctantly, offered a couple of carrots, and observed his subject from outside the stall. The question was who was behind the bars. Coker was okay with my husband Max and me, not affectionate but okay, and I'm ashamed to admit we passively encouraged his rudeness to others.

For supplements, actually substitutes, Anderson asked me to gather some photos of Coker which I did. I think he had envisioned a schmaltzy rendering of a girl and her sweet horse. Wrong. My favorite picture of

Coker was taken by Max at the Farmington Horse Show my sophomore or junior year in college. Farmington was for decades a favorite event held annually the second weekend in May on the Polo Field in Farmington, Connecticut. I remember vaguely but fondly the day Max took the picture Anderson relied on most. Max loved Coker as much as I did and snapped this picture in the morning when I was riding him on the flat. In my mind's eye I can still see the dew on the grass and the shadowy horses and riders cantering in the distance. The reason I know that it was a warm-up hack is that Coker's martingale is tied up at the bottom of the neck. If I used a martingale when riding him on the flat, he hid behind the bridle. If I jumped him without the martingale, he got ahead of the bridle, i.e., too strong for me to regulate his stride. The solution was obvious: tie it up for the flat work—walking, trotting, and cantering—and use it when jumping. I must have had a class coming up early that day with no time to go back to our tent stall to put the martingale on.

Another telling detail is that I am fully dressed to ride into the show ring—hard hat, jacket, stock tie, breeches, and boots. The number on my back is missing; probably Max was holding it for me.

Only a one-horse barn like ours in those days would braid a jumper's mane and tail. Braiding is traditional in the hunter and equitation divisions, but not for the jumpers. We obviously had time on our hands that morning to do all that braiding! I may well have braided some colleagues' horses as well, for even then braiding was a sure way to make some easy money: ten dollars a pop in the '50's, forty in the twenty-first century. (In those days ten or twenty dollars—two manes—would buy dinner; forty might not nowadays.)

In all fairness both Coker and I look better in the portrait than we did in real life. His ugly head was streamlined as were my figure and attire. The artist more than did justice to his muscular body and his shiny coat. On the other hand, he exaggerated the horse's conformation faults (possibly because he did not like the creature that much, having been evicted from his stall. And besides Coker was not his type.) I remember Coker's neck as longer and more swanlike, his shoulders bigger and more sloping. The whole area in front of the rider is shorter in the picture than it was in real life. The artist made him tipping over his front legs which he did, but not to the extent shown. Coker's massive and powerful hindquarters, essential for jumping big fences, are masterfully portrayed.

Along with the horse, this painting was the other part of my dowry when Max and I got married. It was traditionally hung over our couch in every home we've lived in: 518 E. 88th Street, New York City; Old Church Road, North Stanwich Road, Taconic Road, all in Greenwich, Connecticut; and now for the past thirty plus years on Stone Hill Road in Bedford. Mostly unnoticed, it has presided over our home for over forty-five years. Beneath its muted green and shiny brown hues our two boys have grown from newborns to toddlers, to students in grammar school, junior high, high school, college, and graduate school. Now they are both gone to live on their own, far from Coker's distant, indifferent gaze. A succession of dogs have romped and slept near Coker's austere presence: Fritz, then Bullet and Jimmy, Duke, Clay and Bear, Klaus, Sam and Dylan, Pinocchio, Brumbear, Sarah and now Sister, Miracle and Blitz. Pinocchio's eighteen years spanned nearly half the life of the painting itself. This pastel has watched Max and me grow old and grey; it has guarded us in sickness and in health, through all the ups and downs of our lives.

Looking at the faded photograph that Anderson used, from the distance of nearly fifty years I can see he missed a lot, mostly Coker's mischievous expression and cocked ear. The horse's impatiently swishing tail in the photo was refined in the portrait.

When I turn my toes up, this portrait might find its way into the dumpster. Its size alone qualifies it as clutter, and it does not mean anything to anyone but Max and me. For us it embodies a lot of memories: of the horse, the day, a "favorite day," the horse show, and our youth. Were the artist still alive, he probably would not happily recall the eagerly anticipated and fondly remembered day when he came to meet Coker. For our children, grandchildren, and the dogs the picture is little more than wallpaper. Perhaps some equine art enthusiast will snap it up. Anderson is still a pretty famous artist even if the painting itself is not one of his best efforts.

Epilogue: To my delight, my son Phil is enamored of Coker's portrait and it has found a safe home in his bungalow in Wellington, Florida. Fifty years have put some new spins on an old, favorite portrait.

A Treasured Painting: Mr. Coker and The Author in 1961 by C.W. Anderson.

A photograph of Mr. Coker and the Author at
the Farmington Horse Show, 1959,
(photo by Max Richter).

"Three Offers" Comes to Coker Farm

"Three Offers" is a nineteenth-century, faded print of a beautiful, young horsewoman smilingly striding through a muddy river as three pink-coated horsemen attempt to rescue her. In the background, mounted fox hunters are disappearing in the distance, following the hounds. Ever since I could remember, this print has hung over the fireplace reminding our fox hunting family that our favorite sport is hazardous but usually not tragic. The lovely equestrienne is clearly unhurt, and everyone in the picture is smiling.

Imagine my surprise and delight when I visited Christie's Annual Sporting Art Preview in Manhattan where the original painting hung in all its glory about to be auctioned off on the morrow. To my horror no one knew the painting's real name. The plaque on the wall titled it "An Unfortunate Tumble" and in the catalogue it was simply called "The Rescue" and the estimated price was $6,000-$8,000. Extravagant but doable, I thought to myself, and having been stashing money all summer intending to replace my tag-along, two-horse trailer with an upscale goose-neck that was a lot more stable and steady on the highways when big tractor trailers roar past, I could at least afford to think about being extravagant. A yellowish cast reconfirmed a fellow admirer's observation that the painting had clearly been surrounded by smokers much of its one-hundred-plus years. It was tastelessly bound by a heavy, Victorian, gold-leaf frame. I dared to hope all the experts would consider the piece beyond redemption.

Meanwhile, I succumbed to the delight of studying the painting, for many of the details were lost in our faded print, and besides it was no more than unappreciated wallpaper to our busy lives. The horsewoman was impeccably turned out in a proper navy blue habit, complete with the traditional side-saddle skirt, white blouse, and gloves and, perched slightly askew on her head, a bowler. Though her smile cheerfully welcomed her rescuers, she firmly held on to her crop in case they chose to take advantage of her precarious situation. The old gentleman striding toward her in the river has already lost his top hat down stream and has removed his glove in hopes of grasping her more securely. A Victorian expert pointed out to me once long ago that gloves off of Victorian gentlemen was the equivalent of pants off nowadays.

Her horse, a dark dapple grey, (his color clearly visible in the original) is fleeing the scene off to the right, vainly pursued by another swain. Any horse person could easily imagine how the mishap occurred. In contrast to the big, solid white horse stolidly standing in the river to help with the rescue, the dark grey running away was clearly a youngster, for all grey horses start their lives as dark greys and get white with age, no matter how dark they are in their youth. Probably the young miss ignored everyone's advice to ride an old faithful Dobbin instead of the youngster. Surely the rushing river scared the colt who refused to go down the bank, and no doubt she gave him a smack to get him into the water. Frightened, he probably took a flying leap, lost his footing, and fell, dumping her in the process. The two sidesaddle horns make falling off almost impossible, but somehow she managed to extricate herself. In any case, the end result was that she was in the drink, and her mount was gone.

A similar experience was mine a few years ago when I tried to get my colt, Riley, to cross a rushing stream in Lake Placid. Riley balked, I gave him several smacks, and he leapt into the river, slipped, and fell. Luckily he had the decency to wait for me, for there were no swains in pink coats to rescue me. I climbed on a rock, remounted, and rode up and down the river to reassure him that it was okay. Both of us were soaking wet. The next day after a gentle smack he studied the river and marched carefully in.

Another key detail visible in the original was that the girl's safety stirrup popped open in the melee. My son, Hans, always called those alleged "safety stirrups" dangerous stirrups; they let you down just when you really need them. (In all fairness, those stirrups do prevent your foot from getting stuck in the stirrup and your being dragged to your death by a frightened horse.) The jury will always be out, for the stirrup may have saved her from being crushed in the river or, on the other hand, if it had held out, she might not have fallen off at all. Without asking I know my son's opinion on the matter.

On my way home from Christie's I called my younger son, Philip, to tell him about the painting. At once a conservative investor and daring seeker of opportunities, Phil shared my enthusiasm and egged me on to get it, "Just buy it Mom. What an opportunity. One day that painting will be worth a lot more than our dwindling dollars."

The next morning I called Christie's and nervously arranged to bid over the phone. The estimated time for Lot 79, the painting I wanted, was 11 am, give or take, so I distractedly filled the morning riding and giving lessons until my cell phone rang. I fled from the concrete block indoor ring where reception is sketchy and stood outside shivering in our open Grand Prix Field. Having never bought anything at auction, I was surprised to be gripped by auction fever even before the bidding started at $3,000. A couple of bidders in the audience bid it right up over the promised $8,000. Slowly the bids crept up toward $20,000 and the others gave up.

"Going once, Going twice, Sold," and it was mine. The shock was unsettling and still distracted, I finished the morning lessons, scheming when and how I could pick it up. Too big to fit in the car, it would have to be transported in the pick-up. The 8% tax made collecting it in Manhattan a bad idea, so I persuaded a friend in Vermont to receive it, and several days later went off in the pick-up truck to collect it and bring it home.

Luckily, such paintings are removed from their frames for shipping, and when we unpacked the giant, plywood parcel, we left the ugly frame to molder in the garage until two years later. It was sold for over $500, a windfall if ever there was one. Where to hang it was a no-brainer for there was only one wall in the house big enough. My treasured portrait of Mr. Coker was demoted to the spare bedroom, and "Three Offers" hangs un-cleaned and frameless, on the wall of weathered barn siding in the TV room. I love it just the way it is.

Tag-along horse trailers have been good enough for me for fifty years, and going forward, mine will just have to do. I've promised myself to be careful to avoid mishaps. As for the painting, I will leave it to my sons who can have it properly cleaned and framed if they like. If they don't want to keep it, they can sell it on to someone who loves it as much as I do. It won't be hard to find a taker.

Three Offers.
Painted by Alfred W. Strutt, 1897.

VI.

Adventures Off the Farm

More About Three Offers: Still No Offers

My favorite painting, "Three Offers," by Alfred W. Strutt 1897, depicts a beautiful girl whose horse has fallen into a rushing river. Knee deep in water and smiling, she is about to be rescued by three scarlet-coated swains: one on horseback, one leaning from the bank, and the third, a jolly old gent, striding out to fold her into his arms and carry her to safety.

    A faded print of that oil painting has hung over our mantel ever since I could remember, and I had always hoped that if I ever fell off my horse into a river, some gallants, actually one would do, would rescue me. When I was a child, my pony often used to roll in one of the red, muddy tributaries of the mighty Raritan River that run through New Jersey. Usually I rode alone, so after she rudely dumped me she would usually take off for home and leave me to walk the several miles back, water dripping from my pigtails and squishing in my boots. Wet and cold, I was anything but "cool" like the beautiful girl in the painting. Upon approaching my seventieth birthday, I found that over sixty years later there was still no one around to rescue me. During the Lake Placid Horse Show, grey-haired and wrinkled, I climbed on my current pet, Blink, and headed out alone for a trail ride through the lovely mountains that surround the horse show.

    We started down the dark, wooded trail next to the horse show while over the treetops blared the announcer calling exhibitors to the first class of the day. As we descended the hill, his voice became fainter until finally silence drifted over our heads and all around us. When we reached the valley floor, the sound of the rushing river filled our ears. We followed the winding path along the water to the crossing where we plunged in and splashed across. Most horses are reluctant to step into still or surging water, but Blink likes to paw and splash around. Sometimes he drops his nose beneath the surface to blow bubbles and pretend to scare himself. Just a few years before, my frightened, young horse, Riley, had balked, jumped, and then fallen in this very river, dumping me, but he was too terrified to move, so I caught him and rode him unceremoniously back to the horse show. The crossing was rocky, and since I didn't want Blink slamming his feet unnecessarily on the stones, I kicked him across and up the steep bank on the far side. Then we followed a well-groomed trail; I was half-hoping to find a place where Blink could splash around a bit. Several miles down the river I spotted a lovely sandy beach. "Perfect" I thought and headed him into water, which was quite deep, over his knees, and stiller than it had been upstream.

Blink gazed around and started pawing, splashing water over both of us. He put his head down to blow bubbles, and the next thing I knew he dropped like a rock to his knees. The water was swirling over my boots as I spurred and whipped him, determined to make him get back up on his feet. As he rolled over on his side, luxuriating in the refreshing cool water, I jumped off, not wanting to get a broken leg out of this little mishap. After a royal dunking, I stood up waist deep in the no-longer-still water as Blink made his way to the far shore where the river was even deeper. My heart sank as I watched the water rush over the top of my son Philip's favorite saddle.

Blink found the deep water scary and luckily turned to me to rescue him. I had had visions of him galloping home, skidding into the horse show, alarming family and friends. Worse still was my predicament: alone, soaking wet, on foot three to four miles from home/the horse show. No chance to call for help. Surely my saturated iPhone was dead. Even my favorite watch, originally bought in Rome in 1960 for my husband Max was soaked. It was the only watch he ever wore.

I grabbed Blink's dangling reins and led him to the sandy bank which I used as a mounting block to climb back up on him as he stood patiently still. We made our way home, along the river, fording it hastily with me holding Blink's head high, so he would not be tempted to roll again, and then climbing the steep wooded trail back up the mountain to the horse show. Water squished in my boots, on Phil's beloved saddle, everywhere.

We were the laughing stock of our tent as neighbors gathered around to hear my silly story. Blink stood proudly, the center of attention, while the girls scraped the water off his belly and toweled him dry. I poured the water out of my boots, stood them in the sun next to Phil's saddle, my watch and iPhone. By the end of the day none was the worst for wear, or rather for the dunking. We oiled the saddle, and luckily it had several days to regain its former look before the owner appeared. Amazingly, both my watch and iPhone still worked, tributes to ancient and modern technology. My boots are used to getting wet (not soaked though), but they were good to go again as soon as the sun dried them out.

Now I know not to trust Blink in rivers and ponds. No more blowing bubbles, for when the head goes down, the body follows. My pony I had as a child was worse, even with a short rein to keep her head up, she would try to roll any chance she got. Privately, I was quite chuffed that I could still cope with little mishaps. I did not need "three offers" or even one. I caught my horse, climbed on, and rode home. If Blink had deserted me miles from home, I could have walked. I had done it before, but I'm sure glad I didn't have to do it again.

Willard at Saratoga

The first time my brother-in-law, Willard, now a leading race horse trainer, rode steeple chasers at the Saratoga meeting in August, he had to lie about his age to get on the track, let alone ride. Willard grew up in Aiken, South Carolina and the New York tracks—Belmont, Aqueduct and Saratoga—were the center of horse racing in America. "If you can make it there, you can make it anywhere," as Frank Sinatra was singing on the radio. In those days, and even today, to ride over jumps at Saratoga was a big deal and all was well until the last race of the meeting when to quote Willard:

"My horse fell, and I got my bell rung. When I woke up in the hospital ten days later, everyone had left. Everyone—riders, trainers, groomers—had gone back to Belmont or Aqueduct.

The hospital staff took up a collection to buy him a ticket on the Greyhound bus back to New York. He was probably not the only kid they gave a "leg up" to over the years. They also got him some clothes since all he had to wear were his racing silks that he had on when he fell.

Sitting alone in the bus on his way back to New York, Willard must have figured out for himself the old adage, "what doesn't kill you makes you stronger." Love of the sport still gives him the determination to get up every morning at 3:30 am even though he is now in his seventies. Never one to forget where he came from and who helped him along the way, he is glad to give "a leg up" to anyone who needs and deserves it.

Fifty years later Willard is a leading race horse trainer and proud owner of a beautiful farm, but it did not come easily: first he rode races, later he trained. A lot of race riders "get their bell rung" once too often and they end up as grooms living in little rooms at the track, "on the backstretch." Taking care of a couple of horses is all they can manage. Willard not only survived; he prevailed. He is still a leading race horse trainer.

Racing Our Car

This story, a knock off of young Patrick Smithwick's memoir, *Racing My Father*, about his dad, Patrick Smithwick, one of the great steeplechase jockeys, is told by my brother-in-law, J. Willard Thompson, who also rode chasers in those days.

    The race in Paddy's old Chevy started after the morning workouts at Belmont and a couple of "pops" at Esposito's. Paddy and Willard quickly pulled on their sweat suits in the parking lot outside the bar; they both had to be five pounds lighter by the time they got to Monmouth for the 3:00 pm steeplechase, and they were late. Their "hot car" was already baking in the July noon sun. While Paddy started the car and turned on the heater, they each took a swig from the sweating gallon jug of screwdrivers and shaved ice that sat between them. Hot cars are torture, but they enable jockeys to lose weight quickly. With the heat on high and the windows rolled up, wrapped in rubber sweat suits, Paddy and Willard were good to go and likely to make the weight when they got there. The jug of chilled screwdrivers and countless cigarettes deadened the pain a little.

    Everything went according to plan until they got to the Garden State Parkway, virtually a parking lot that afternoon. Paddy glanced over at the wide open grassy meridian and said to Willard, "Hang on, boy. Here we go." When Paddy had to get somewhere, he went directly to it. That's how he won races. They bumped along for a mile or so on the grass past astonished drivers stalled in their air-conditioned cars. All too soon, the inevitable happened; a cop pulled them over, lights flashing and siren wailing. Willard slid the slippery jug of screwdrivers down between his feet. Paddy cracked his window to pass his license and registration to the big beefy fellow outside, apologizing sincerely, "Sorry, officer. This is a hot car 'cause we each have to lose five pounds before the chase at Monmouth this afternoon. And we're late."

The officer grunted, looked at his licenses and exploded, "JesusChristPaddySmithwick.

"Yes, sir, and not very proud of it right now."

"You got a winner this afternoon?"

"Well, sir, he's a nice horse and we could get lucky. I'd say you're safe to bet him on the nose," meaning bet him to win.

"Okay," the cop replied and slid the license and registration back through the slit in the window. "I'll escort you down over the bridge. You know the shortcut from the first exit on the other side?"

"Yes, sir we always go that way."

And so they were off, tailgating the cop with lights flashing and siren wailing. They got there on time, made the weight, and Paddy won. The horse's name was Police Car. I hope the cop bet on him.

Riding in the Maryland Hunt Cup

Dr. Danny Marks, my good friend, tells a great Paddy-Smithwick story on himself. When he was in vet school at the University of Pennsylvania in the fifties, he fell in with the steeplechase crowd in Pennsylvania and Maryland. The Maryland Hunt Cup is a grueling four mile race over timber, the "timber" being more than twenty split rail fences, many over five feet high. Some say it is the toughest race in the world to survive, let alone win. The Smithwick family was at the top of their game, so when someone offered Danny a horse to ride in the Maryland Hunt Cup, he sought Paddy out for advice. Since Danny spent most of his time in those days studying, he knew he was not in great physical shape.

Danny asked Paddy, "What's the best way to get fit to ride in the Maryland Hunt Cup? Do you lift weights, jog, or just gallop a lot of horses?"

"What horse are you riding?" was Paddy's question. When Danny told him, he answered, "How fit do you have to be to jump two fences. You're going to fall at the third." The third fence is the first real test; from where the horses take off, it is 5'3" to 5'6" high. Like all men, Danny didn't want to hear what he couldn't do, so he trained rigorously all winter long: lifting weights, jogging, riding his bike.

Race day dawned clear and cool. Eight horses went to the post. Danny's mount jumped the first two fences well, and just as Paddy predicted, fell at the third. To jump a five foot plus obstacle at breakneck speed requires a horse of extraordinary courage and scope. Danny's steed had the courage but not the scope, so he hit the top rail with his knees and they tipped over. Luckily both of them walked away from it. Danny gave up steeple chasing and became an outstanding veterinarian, one of the best in the country.

John Kingery:
Big Owner at the Quarter Horse World Championships

John Kingery's finest hour as a show jumper owner was when his horse, Mr. Bar Do Too, won the Jumper Jackpot ($3,000) at the Quarter Horse World Championships in Columbus, Ohio, in the late '70's.

Larking around the Greenwich countryside, John accidentally discovered that Bart could jump. On the far side of a big, open field was a formidable stone wall next to a locked gate. Always a chancer, John galloped Bart toward the wall, and they cleared it with ease. (Bart's father, Three Bars, was a well-known sire of Quarter Horse Jumpers, but the Kingerys were big into barrel racing; Audrey and Bart were third in the country one year.) That afternoon John went to the tack store and bought an English saddle. The horn on his Western saddle got in his way, he told the cute salesgirl with a wicked wink. From then on there was no stopping the pair; they jumped every stone wall in Greenwich and were never deterred by the fields turning into lawns as suburbia encroached.

One year John took it into his head that he wanted to show Bart at the Quarter Horse Congress. Luckily I was able to convince him that if he wanted the little horse to have a chance to win, we needed a "real rider," not John "geeing and hawing" and flopping around on his back.

John was enamored of my rider, Ellie Raidt, and loved the idea of her riding the horse. We agreed, pending two conditions: Ellie and I would have the horse with us in training for two weeks before the event and Audrey, his wife, would come with us to Columbus to make sure there were no awkward situations. We took Bart along with us to the Harrisburg Horse Show to practice a little (and to pull his mane and trim his whiskers!) John and Audrey blew in with their one-horse trailer, scooped up Bart and Ellie and took off speeding to Columbus. Fearing for my life, I went by air.

The competition was at night in a very small arena packed to the ceiling with a screaming crowd. Luckily Bart was a cool dude, the only one on our team. John was making us all crazy, so we sent him out of the schooling area. There were two short standards, two rails, and no jump cups, so Audrey and I held the rail for Bart and Ellie to warm up over. In hopes of making their horses careful, the cowboys were throwing rails at them as they jumped. Little Bart was a super careful jumper, so the last thing he needed was to get a smack in the schooling area. In the ring the course was four verticals, two on each side of the arena, and a triple bar down the middle, twice around and finish over the gigantic triple bar. The verticals—two rails each—were at least 4'6" high and the triple bar just as high and 6' wide.

We knew Bart had to jump a big schooling fence so he would not be surprised in the ring. For Bart's last warm-up jump, Audrey who is not very tall was holding the rail up over her head. Bart and Ellie cantered into the ring, focused on the job at hand despite the clamor all around them. Bart jumped around beautifully; Ellie gave him a lovely ride. A clear round, the crowd roared, and they were eligible for the jump off against the clock: once around and down the middle. There were eight in the jump off, and we were fifth to go. Holly Caristo was the first and blazed around in twenty-six seconds. In the schooling area, Audrey stood on her tiptoes as she held the rail as high as she could. John was screaming from the sidelines. Bart and Ellie flew around clear in twenty-four seconds. No one could catch us. In the winners' circle John collected a brand new saddle and the check for $3,000. The rest I don't remember, for we all got drunk celebrating after tucking dear Bart into bed.

West Palm Beach:
The Ups and Downs of Show Jumping

Recently we were once again reminded of the ups and downs of show jumping. It started like a normal day with Philip up early to hack his two jumpers in the dark before his 8 am class at the horse show in West Palm Beach. The sun was just rising among the palm trees as I led Kondor out the back gate over to the horse show.

This was as good as it gets, horse showing in sunny Florida, where so far the weather has been perfect. Flowers were blooming and birds were singing as we sauntered over to the deNemethy ring where brightly painted jumps on state-of-the-art, all-weather footing awaited us.

"It feels like a favorite day in the making," I thought to myself and so it was, sort of. We walked the course, Kondor and Phil warmed up well over some schooling jumps, and cantered into the ring. They started fine over the first few jumps, but the triple combination, three jumps close to each other, looked like a lot of lumber to Kondor who needed a kick in the ribs to keep him going. Instead Phil sat still, which is what Kondor usually likes. Kondor stuttered, Phil fell off, sliced his chin, and bit his tongue. As he walked out of the ring, he looked like the victim of an attempted axe murder. Blood was dripping all over his white shirt and breeches. He said his jaw was not broken; we mopped up the blood and put him on the trusty Glasgow, who recently retired from International Grand Prix competition to the amateur ring. He is more than a good horse; he is a great horse who can be counted on to rise to the occasion. Still bleeding, Phil hopped the horse over a couple of low jumps in the schooling area.

I'm fine," he announced, and Norman advised him to have a nice canter around (it was a one-round speed class) for the morrow when they would compete in the classic in the big ring.

In they went, still dripping blood, jumped a clear round, quickly as it turned out, and won in a class of sixty-five entries, which, of course, took the sting out of the various injuries. Leaving Sarah to rinse the blood out of Glasgow's mane and put him away, we went directly from the Winner's Circle to the emergency room to stitch up Phil's wounds.

Not exactly a favorite day, but it could have been so much worse. Once again we survived the ups and downs of show jumping thanks to our generous Glasgow, who proceeded to give us a real favorite day on Sunday. He jumped double clear rounds in the classic over a very big course in the International Arena, placed second of sixty-five by two tenths of a second, and having amassed the most points, was Champion. We hoped for more ups and no downs the next week.

VII.

Road Trips

Roads Often Taken

"How much can come, how much can go, and yet abide the world"

For over sixty years I have been taking a road, actually many roads, to our family farm at the top of a mountain far away in Vermont. Most of the journeys have been thankfully uneventful, forgettable and hence forgotten, but some are engraved in my soul.

The many almost forgotten trips usually started in the late afternoon with Max and our two sons, Hans and Philip, or early evening: after work, school, a horse show, whatever. The object was to get there as soon as possible, and we drove as if we were carriage horses with blinders on, staring only at the road unrolling in front of our feet/wheels. Those trips were mostly a blur, even the quick, half-halts at Friendly's in Greenfield to get ice-cream and let the dogs out to pee.

The very first journey in 1947 was memorable mostly because it was long, over twelve hours. In those days there were no super highways between New Jersey, our winter home, and Vermont, our new summer farm. Our brand new, canvas-topped Willy's Jeep was well able for the trip, and, as it turned out, so were we. My mother drove. Her mother, our grandmother then in her 70's, rode shotgun. My sister and I sat behind, across from each other, on the metal benches with our three dogs at our feet. Behind us was the two-horse trailer my father built himself, loaded with one horse and our pony as well as a lot of miscellaneous, fragile and carefully-packed dishes and knickknacks for the new/old farm. The brave, little Jeep murmured all the way up the long hills, "I think I can, I think I can" like *The Little Engine That Could.* My grandmother had packed snacks, so the only stops were to fill the gas tank and drain the plumbing, ours and the dogs'. We left at dawn and arrived just before dark. Everything in between is long since forgotten except for our hard seats and endless questions, "Are we there yet?" Finally we were "there," followed a few days later by our father who borrowed a cattle truck and shipped the rest of the horses cross-ways head and tail. They arrived scrambled but basically unscathed. Other childhood journeys were not remarkable.

Meanwhile our new/old farm became more habitable with the addition of running water, electricity, a telephone, and finally even central heating. My next memorable journey was in the late '50's in the dead of winter with Max, my new boyfriend, later husband of nearly fifty years. In his trusty, little, ancient Volkswagen, he picked me up after dark at college halfway between Manhattan and our destination, "Peri Wahn," ("Journey's End" in Persian, well-named). Interstate 91 was on the drawing board then, so we had to advance slowly for four hours up the torturous Route 5. As we went north, the walls of snow on both sides of the road grew taller, and my heart misgave me, for I knew we would have to walk up the last, long hill. I silently scolded myself, "This is no way to treat an adorable new boyfriend."

Sure enough the road was not plowed, and we had to stagger through waist high snow up the long, last mile. The little, red house sparkled in the moonlight, but I warned Max not to be dazzled, for I knew it was ice cold inside. Long before carbon footprints were a concern, my parents drained the plumbing, shut off the heat, and closed the house for the winter for purely economic reasons; it would have cost a couple of hundred dollars to keep it open for the odd visit. This was indeed the odd visit. The lock on the door was frozen, and we had to crawl through the basement window. Luckily Max loved the place, and it was the first of many trips north for the next fifty years.

Imagine our delight the very next fall when we discovered that Interstate 91 stretched all the way from Hartford to White River Junction shortening our journey to four hours instead of six. Even the rest areas were there just for us. (In Massachusetts they are called "rest areas;" in Vermont they are "parking areas," even today.) Our favorite was the one just beyond the "Welcome to Vermont" sign on the highway; it is closed now. When we couldn't keep our hands off each other any longer we'd stop and neck for a while.

The most exciting part of our weekly winter trips North in my college years was the last mile up the hill. Would the road be plowed or would we have to walk carrying a minimum of provisions? Even if the road was plowed, we had to put chains on Max's rusty, old VW, never fun in the cold and the dark. Sometimes we slid into the ditch, so besides packing a flashlight and gloves, we had to remember a shovel. Even with chains on the car, we had to get up momentum in the valley and drive up the hill at breakneck speed, bouncing off the walls of snow on each side of the road. Occasionally we ended up in the ditch which meant we had to dig out, back all the way down and try again.

The old VW was a tough car; it took a lot of abuse during those college years. It balked when the temperature was lower than 10° below zero; it would refuse to start. But Max was resourceful; on frigid mornings he lovingly warmed the engine, particularly the oil, with an old hairdryer we found in the closet. We soon improved on that tactic, and while we unpacked at night, Max would drain the oil into a pot which we'd warm and put back in the car the next morning. Luckily it did not get super cold that often.

One memorable journey home was in the winter when the children were small. After a long day of skiing, all four of us and the dog piled into the VW, skis strapped to the back, pointing toward heaven. Philip, our youngest, still a toddler, cried all the way home for no reason whatsoever that we could figure out. We survived even that and were good to go again the very next weekend.

In recent years Thanksgiving at the farm has become a tradition, a great time to gather the family but not a good time to travel. Heavy traffic made our four-hour trip six or seven hours. Often we were plagued by rain and fog, even sleet and snow sometimes. Meanwhile Alzheimer's was fogging Max's brain, so the topics of conversation were limited to weather. (He always had a pilot's interest in the weather); the wonderful "new" road, (Interstate 91, by then forty-years-old); and the "new" speed limit of 65, (by then five-years-old.) Those were trips I am trying to forget, but, on the other hand, I would give anything to be driving up 91 again with Max by my side exclaiming about the weather, the road, the speed limit. I would bite my lip as I responded companionably to his observations. Now when I see couples arguing or even bickering in airports, on planes or trains, I want to shake them and tell them, "shut up, you don't know how lucky you are to have each other." Long an observer of couples, I used to be at once thankful and scornful. Max had such a good disposition, it rubbed off on me, and we did not bicker or fight ever. Now my scorn has turned to anger, and I just want to shake those crabby couples.

This time accompanied only by a couple of dogs, I had no desire to hurry. I left early in the morning so I could enjoy the scenery and some side trips as well. All the way the road was wide open, and I self indulgently dawdled along stopping for breakfast in Westport with son Hans and family, in New Haven to drive by my cousin's old house, scene of harmless debauchery during our teens, for Yale was nearby. Next came Hartford, its lovely, tall, glass building peeking over the treetops as I traveled up Interstate 91. I passed the big, blue onion, perched on the old, abandoned brick warehouse and thought of Wallace Stevens, sometime Hartford insurance agent and all-time great American poet. Next I went on to Northampton, past the Ox Bow, a u-shaped bend in the Connecticut River where the locals and some college friends keep their boats. Fond memories are there too, the most vivid being the time I accidentally dumped Mr. Mendenhall, our college president and avid sailor, in the drink. On our way to Vermont the summer after graduation when my friend and I stopped to see him, he was about to go sailing on the Ox Bow and would we like to come along. Of course. To make a long story short, I stepped into the dingy before he had a chance to get to the other side of it. I jumped nimbly back on to the dock, but he went down heavily with his "ship." When he surfaced, sputtering good-naturedly he echoed my own thoughts: "Good thing I've graduated."

At Smith in Northampton I was eager to check out the brand new riding ring. I was instrumental in raising money for, (my only effort to date for the alma mater). It is a fine addition to a very good training facility. Reunion classes were just moving out of the dorms, so I had a chance to revisit my old room where I lived for four years: a plain, slightly pie shaped rectangle with a big window overlooking the "Quad," the quadrangle of dorms. The bed, desk and chair looked very much like the ones I had. If they were the same ones, I hope the bed had a new mattress at least! I was glad to see everything looked the same, one "still point in a turning world."

My next visit was to say a quick hello to Shaina, my friend of thirty years, and her family in Granby, near Amherst. My first and best working student, she helped me organize our new farm in the summer of '78. Like a Duracell battery, she is still a bundle of energy. She proudly showed me around their newly built stable. My next stop was at the used book store off 91, a three floors and basement Victorian house chock full of books. I wandered vaguely around, bought nothing, and continued to Friendly's in Greenfield, our traditional stop for decades. I let the dogs out, grabbed an ice cream cone and continued.

An hour later up 91, looming ahead in the glorious spring sunshine was the awesome pyramid, Ascutney Mountain, reminding me that I had unconsciously taken notice of the mountains along the way: Sleeping Giant in New Haven where we enjoyed some picnics in the '50's and Mt. Tom in Northampton which featured night skiing during the week. Because my college friend Betty and I had skier boyfriends, we had to practice several times during the week in an effort to keep up with them and not lose them due to clumsiness.

A favorite journey to Peri Wahn from a different direction was the annual one between the two Lake Placid horse shows, across Lake Champlain on the lofty bridge and through the open meadows of the Champlain Valley, presided over by a once-abandoned, now renovated, awesome Victorian house. I next traveled on to Ripton, Robert Frost country. I often stopped for a sandwich and soda at the general store and enjoyed a picnic on the rock in front of Frost's cabin, weather permitting. The Breadloaf School of English, a mecca for poets and writers, where I once attended a Robert Frost seminar, holds fond memories for me as well. From there it was downhill to Barnard where I admired the crystalline Silver Lake and picked up some groceries. For many years Max would come to the farm for a couple of days of R&R, more favorite days for both of us until he had to go back to work and I back to the horse show.

This time on leaving Interstate 91, I noticed the lilac bushes were in bloom by every home, even the poor shacks, along the road. It was "lilac heaven" in Vermont this time of year. I took the bumpy, dirt road shortcut around Ascutney, as usual arousing the dogs who thought we were "there," but they soon settled down. I decided it was a perfect day to visit "Twenty Foot," a hidden waterfall and pool where Max and I often used to skinny dip and picnic. Well known and loved by locals but still undiscovered by tourists, it hides in the woods, the water way too cold for swimming or even wading this time. My next stop was in South Woodstock where the Green Mountain Horse Association was in full swing, full of trailers, people, and horses in for the Memorial Day Trail Ride. I greeted the few people I knew and went on to Woodstock where my car refused to pass Gillingham's General Store that sells the best smoked cheese in the world. I also visited the Yankee Bookshop, known for their traditional and eclectic books. To my delight I found a "new" (1991) biography of Robert Frost. Perfect reading for a lonesome Vermont weekend.

Only once have I come to Peri Wahn during "mud season," most of April and the early part of May. The hook for me then was that the road up the hill was "almost impossible." I took the bait and tried it, throwing the car into low gear and gunning it up just like we used to in the snow in the old days. The road was rough and rutted with water rushing down everywhere. Trying to keep out of the ruts, I settled for the muck and pressed the accelerator to the floor, expecting at each bend in the road to land in the ditch, as by now the machine was half out of control. Suddenly, we were at the top, the car panting like an exhausted horse and driver heaving a sigh of relief.

By the end of May mud season is over. The town has been working on our road with their graders and gravel, so it was like a boulevard. I reached the top of the world, where lilacs were blooming all around the house and barn. It was "lilac heaven" this week as the sun was setting, and I settled in for a quiet weekend at Peri Wahn. I am wondering if I will remember this lovely, leisurely trip through the spring sunshine in two, or five, or ten years. I think I will.

Columbus Day Weekend

My annual Columbus Day weekend sojourn to the dear and dilapidated old family farm in Vermont was fraught with more adventure than usual. Basically it was a lovely, glorious time echoing more than fifty years of good fun, but this year I was broadsided by some bad luck and bad judgment. I left Thursday afternoon in an effort to beat the "leaf peepers" who surely would be out in droves on Friday to admire the glorious foliage up north. The long drive gave me plenty of time to reminisce. In the early days when I was in college, after work Max picked me up at school in Northampton, halfway there, and we jostled along the windy, old Route 5, arriving around midnight. I don't remember a single rainy weekend, for we always grabbed an extra day, Monday, in hopes that Smith College, my alma mater, would celebrate the unique and best holiday of the year, "Mountain Day." On that glorious day the bells would peel at 8 am, classes were cancelled for the day, and students were encouraged to enjoy the world around them/us. And indeed we did, and we maintained that tradition long after college.

As our family grew, we brought them along to enjoy life at the farm. One by one children, dogs, and horses joined us. It became a major event involving much planning. Max's mother, Oma, made sure she would arrive from Germany for her annual visit in time to come with us. Max drove the horse van loaded with two horses, two ponies, and all their feed and gear. Usually Hans went with him. Phil kept Oma and me and the various dogs company in whatever can we had at the time. We took an extra day or two off from work and school celebrating our own "Mountain Day." I remember fondly the long rides over the neighboring hills and the cozy evenings in front of the fire—bright, blazing, and warm on the chilly, dark evenings.

Inevitably the kids went off to college, and Oma was too old to travel from Germany, so it was just us and the animals which was fine too: days on horseback and evenings by the fire. Sometimes friends joined us, but for the most part we found that like Max's mentor, Hans Hinrichs, we were "least alone when all alone."

This year the journey itself was uneventful, especially considering I had four lively dogs with me in the pickup truck and my big horse, Blink, in the trailer behind. I tied Blitz, the German shorthaired pointer, securely in the back seat, so he could not jump into my lap and obscure my view of the road. The Jack Russells—grandmother, Sister; mother, Miracle; and almost one-year-old pup, Popcorn—bounced around the cab as we merrily drove along. We stopped briefly in Greenfield at Friendly's for all of us to pee and for me to grab my traditional ice cream. Back on the road in the gathering darkness, the dogs settled down, and we drove on in silence until we left the pavement and continued the last leg of the journey on bumpy dirt roads that always awoke the dogs, now slobbering with excitement, for they knew we were almost "there."

The diesel truck moaned and groaned but gamely and slowly made it up the long, steep hill. By then the moon was guiding us to our jewel of a farm sparkling in the moonlight. I paused for a moment to enjoy the silver stillness before letting the yowling dogs out. They took off in search of adventure while I unloaded Blink and put him away in the snug little barn.

Suddenly a terrible screaming echoed from the woods across the hills. "Uh oh," I thought. "A bear? What could it be?" Then nothing but an awful silence surged back as I called and called, "Sister, Miracle, Popcorn, Blitz."

Finally Sister appeared sheepishly wagging her tail. She seemed fine and soon the others followed. They were not fine. Miracle and Popcorn were covered with porcupine quills. For fifty years we had not had porcupine problems, but I remember when I was a child, there were often porcupine attacks. In all fairness, the dogs always did the attacking. If you leave porcupines alone, they will leave you alone. Clearly the Jack Russells only knew "Attack" and paid the penalty. As always, Sister stood safely back and let the other two jump into the fray.

Back they came to me, a ragged little band, Miracle and Popcorn full of quills and clearly quite shaken. I knew from the old days it was important to get the quills out before they migrated to vital organs and ultimately killed the host. The quills have little fishhooks at the end that goes into the flesh, so removing them is extremely painful, a lot of blood and torn flesh. In the kitchen I set to work, hogtied Miracle, and started yanking out the quills with a pair of good strong pliers. At first she fought me, but soon she realized I was trying to help and lay reasonably still. The kitchen floor was a blood bath, but finally we were done. Next, Popcorn. He went nuts when I tried to tie him up. Clearly there was no way.

"How am I going to find a vet at this hour?" I asked myself, thumbing through the Yellow Pages. I did find a willing victim, and we agreed to meet at the clinic in Woodstock, 10 miles away, at 11 pm. She was a real trouper, and we seemed to be on the right track until I made a couple of dumb decisions.

Since time was of the essence, I decided not to unhitch the trailer and let it tag along. Then instead of backing and turning around in the area in front of the barn, I drove into the nearby paddock to make a quick swing around and be gone. Bad idea. The truck sank to its hubcaps in the muck, and there was no way. Then I decided to unhitch the trailer and leave it there. In my confusion I could not get the jack to go down. By then frantic I lifted the trailer off the ball on the truck and set it on a cinderblock. Amazed at my own strength, I jumped into the truck but to no avail. Even 4-wheel drive could not get us out. Finally I had to give up, call the vet at 11:30 and explain I'd be there in the morning. She was gracious and cheerful, telling me not to worry.

I settled Popcorn as comfortably as possible in an easy chair, took some Advil and a hot bath to persuade my back not to collapse, dozed intermittently until dawn and called Steve, our neighbor, at 6 am to come pull me out. He was just about to leave the house for work and came quickly, changing my luck from bad to good. He cheerfully hauled me out, and I was off to the vet's. I felt I was leaving Popcorn in good hands, went back to the farm and restlessly called for updates all day long. Having once lost a horse to anesthesia for "minor surgery," I am always uneasy when anyone, human or animal, is put under. There was no way to relax and enjoy the glorious weather; even a pleasant ride through the woods on Blink could not calm my nerves. I kept busy fixing fences, bringing in firewood, gathering sticks on the lawn for kindling. Finally after three hours of surgery and a healthy bill, Popcorn was ready to come home in triumph wearing a bonnet on his neck to keep him from chewing his multitudinous stitches. The vet had to cut him from stem to stern, peel back the skin, and remove countless, quills from between his ribs; they were already migrating toward his heart, lungs, and other vital organs.

"A stitch in time saves nine," she remarked cheerfully and sent us happily home to fall into bed exhausted.

The next day friends arrived with two dogs and a horse in tow to celebrate autumn with us, a tradition begun several years before and always delightful. Long, lovely rides and fireside chats made time fly by. Popcorn improved every day.

Monday morning dawned clear and cold, in fact, too cold for my diesel pickup which refused to start. Luckily my friend and neighbor, Steve, rescued us yet again and sent us on our way to near disaster at the dog vet's, where Popcorn had to check in to have drains removed from his elbow before heading home. I parked the truck and trailer loaded with dogs and horse ready to go directly south. I decided to leave the engine running for fear it would not start again, threw it into "Park," but I neglected to engage the emergency brake.

The near disaster started to happen in slow motion. As the vet was removing Popcorn's drains, we glanced out the window watching my dogs raging at a dog passing by on his way into the clinic. Apparently they dislodged the gear shift, for suddenly the pickup and trailer started moving down and across Route 4. We ran, Mindy, the tech assistant, faster than I, out the door and across the road. She sprang into the truck and stopped it just before it hit the house across the busy highway. Whew! How lucky can I be? Not a single scratch on the vehicles, my animals or the many families of "leaf peepers" passing by.

At least now I know I have a strong heart, for if ever there was a heart attack moment, that was it. Thankful to whoever may have been watching over us, I enjoyed an uneventful drive home. "How much can come, how much can go and yet abide the world . . ." and how quickly all can change from good to bad and back again. It's far better to be born lucky than smart or talented or rich.

Our Trip to Lagrangeville

News of an enticing little schooling show for jumpers upcountry came over the Internet. My friend, Nick and my older son Hans, would agree an enticing horse show is an oxymoron, having spent much of their youth hanging around such events. Sam, my up-and-coming twelve-year-old protégé thought it sounded great, a perfect place to start with his new jumper, Seignoir Joe. Proof of Sam's dedication is that he perseveres in a sport largely populated by giggling young girls.

Being totally "dialed in," as all kids are nowadays, he found the Crosswinds website, downloaded the list of classes, the schedule, the directions, everything we needed to know. He even consulted his mother's GPS and found out it would take an hour to get there. The classes we were interested in started at noon, two classes where the fences were 3' high and two where they were 3'6" high. It all sounded too good to be true. A phone call to a friend up that way assured us the ring was lovely, one of those giant bubbles like we've seen over tennis courts, "the footing is excellent, the courses, inviting."

"Let's go," we agreed. No reason not to.

During the week before, we were lucky; all the other riders on the farm were enjoying the balmy weather outdoors, so we had the indoor ring to ourselves to practice riding inside in a smaller area where the jumps come up quickly. On Wednesday we practiced over some low jumps in a couple of simple patterns; Thursday, bigger jumps with some more complex and demanding tracks; Friday, again, bigger jumps, but easier patterns to make sure horse and rider felt like King Kong. They did, and we were good to go.

That night Sam bathed and bandaged Joe, so he'd be ready to go in the morning. We hitched up the pickup and the trailer. He filled the hay-net and packed all his gear (carefully checking our old horse show list to make sure he didn't forget anything): saddle, saddle-pad, boots, girth, bridle, martingale, brushes, rub rags, liniment, a water pail, carrots to reward good behavior and Sam's helmet, crop and spurs. The next day he would wear his breeches, and boots, shirt and tie, and bring his jacket, carefully packed in a hanging bag. Also I reminded him to bring his homework in case there were a lot of entries and we had to hang around for hours waiting for our classes. He gave me the "Aw, shucks" look and I answered,

"Gotta keep your grades up if you want your parents to keep supporting your riding," and he nodded agreeably.

Sam's house was right on the way to the horse show, so I told him I'd load Joe and pick him up at 9:45. While I rode a couple of horses beforehand, the grooms fed and brushed Joe. Then I called Sam to alert him to be out on the road for easy pickup. Sure enough, as I rounded the bend, there he was, bright and eager, with his hanging bag and backpack of books. He seemed taller than I remembered him from yesterday. Has he grown overnight? He is making a habit of getting taller every day. His long boots and short sweater added to the illusion. Just your good-looking, clean-cut kid, his eyes glistening behind his studious glasses, he was clearly ready for a good day of adventure. Having not driven the pickup often lately and having no mechanical aptitude, I put him on to adjusting the heat and finding 8:50 am, my favorite radio station; the golden oldies. He politely admitted his mom listened to old songs and he liked them too.

Sam has a great, natural way about him; he is way beyond his twelve years, but in a real good way. Driving along, I never felt I had to make conversation with him. When we weren't talking, our silences were companionable while we proceeded North on 684 to Route 22 and finally turned onto 55 West. As we got closer I realized that "Crosswinds" in Lagrangeville, N.Y., was the old Rock Bottom Farm, famous for housing and training brilliant horses and riders in the '60's and '70's. I explained the history of the place, for a while home to more than a few international show jumping champions. The one I knew best was the one I started, the well-named tall, dark brown Sympatico. When he was in my barn he was only four or five years old and his owner was a young, inexperienced rider. For several years I cantered him around in some easy, inviting jumper classes, and I never let his owner jump him higher than 3'6". He clearly wanted to be a wonder horse; intelligent and calm, he always focused on the jump and, what we now call "super careful," never touched any fence.

He clearly needed time to develop his skills and his confidence. Such a sensitive and talented horse is easily ruined by rushing his career, jumping too high and too fast and scaring him.

Eventually the owner rightly became eager to progress more quickly and relocated to Rock Bottom Farm and trainer Carl Knee. By then Tico was ready to move up, and Carl persuaded the owner to let the world-class rider Anthony d'Ambrosio show him. His meteoric career is almanacked in the annals of show jumping; among countless other triumphs the horse still holds the high jump record in Madison Square Garden. I knew in my heart I was, as much as anyone, instrumental in developing his career, for an impatient expert could have easily ruined him.

That said, I turned my thoughts to our own tiny triumphs which could some day become another brilliant career but said nothing to the aspiring young rider beside me. Behind us in the trailer was a smart, old horse, well able to jump 3'6"-4', high enough for his young, inexperienced and talented rider, and ahead of us was a day of horse showing at a fine facility over a pattern of jumps just right for Sam's current level of riding.

We turned into the familiar, old entrance to the farm and found ourselves in the wrong place, a tight place, as it turned out, a narrow, little road to the old barn built around a courtyard. It was charming but hard to get turned around in, to go back out and farther down the road to "the real entrance." I've driven horse trailers all my life, but not much lately, and I haven't turned one around in years. If you don't do it just right, trailers have a mind of their own and go merrily in just the direction you don't want them to. If you press the issue, the thing jackknifes and there you are, stuck. Luckily we had plenty of time and after much backing and filling, I got the beast turned around, and we continued down the road to our unmistakable destination, the big bubble on the left, the indoor ring.

We carefully parked in a place where I didn't have to turn around and went over to the ring to check it out. An incredible edifice, it looked as big as a football field from the inside, dotted with an array of freshly painted jumps. After looking it all over, I sent Sam back to tack Joe up while I made the entries at the secretary's stand and exchanged pleasantries with some of the horsy-faced kibitzers I recognized at the ingate.

Luckily the horse show was not swamped with entries, so our first class would start at noon as scheduled. We would not have to hang around for hours waiting and then drive home after dark, but we could take our time getting ready. When I got back to the trailer, Sam had Joe tacked up and led him to the trailer bumper to get on. Having not actually shown Joe before, we weren't sure how excited he would be at a competition even though his previous trainer assured me he'd be "fine." Sam walked, trotted and cantered him around the outdoor warm-up ring and not surprisingly the old boy was calm, cool and collected. After hacking him fifteen to twenty minutes, we stuffed him back in the trailer, so we could walk the course and get a feel of the ring and the questions the course designer was asking.

As we paced off the distances between the jumps, I was delighted to find there were no tricks, no half strides between the fences—four of our strides to one horse stride and all distances were multiples of four. Excellent, I thought. Hit a good lick on the warm-up circle and canter around. Just what we need today; no complicated questions yet.

During the break I seized the opportunity to lead Joe around the ring, so he could have a look at the place while Sam grabbed a sandwich. That done, I gave Sam a leg up and set a practice jump in the schooling area, gradually making it higher and wider as they hopped back and forth over it.

Standing at the ingate, I could not help nervously wondering if the old horse would spook and shy or calmly canter around over the jumps. As they circled in the ring before starting, I could see right away that Joe knew his job, and sure enough he just purred around the course. No fences were knocked down, so they went on to the jump off, medium speed and medium turns as we had agreed, no risky recklessness this early in Sam's career. They finished without faults and ended up third; two "rabbits" went faster, and that was fine. The second and third classes were uneventful replays of the first, and the pair was third again and then second. In the last class the jumps were bigger, a full 3'6", and medium fast in the jump off was good enough to win. When the jumps got bigger the "rabbits" either slowed up a bit or tore the fences down. Inordinately pleased with ourselves, we untacked and blanketed Joe. Then we wrapped his legs, loaded him in the trailer, said our goodbyes and thanks, and headed home trailing clouds of glory and contemplating rosy dreams ahead.

As we savored our fries and ice cream heading home, we also savored our tiny triumphs of the day: I did arrange to get the trailer turned around, Sam rode well, Joe jumped well, and . . . we won, the icing on the cake. Even without the icing, the cake was more than sufficient. Looking back over the years as we drove down 684, I sensed a *déjà vu*. How many times over my almost fifty years in the game, the horse

Sam Johnston and Seignor Joe.

business, have I savored these tiny triumphs. In a way they are more precious that some of the bigger victories that come later, for "well begun is half done."

PS When Sam read this he said, "You forgot the most important part. We won fifty five dollars!" The first prize money he ever won. (His dad was pleased too.)

"Go West, Young Man, Go West"

My son Hans and I set off early one summer morning for California, with the animals carefully tucked in behind us: Tango, Margot's lizard in the very back comfortably warm on his heated rock, plugged into a cigarette lighter, the dogs, Lizzie and Wendel behind us, ears flapping out the window. Hans was at the wheel, and I rode shotgun with a "Playmate" cooler full of nibbles for the journey. As we pulled out of the farm, I thought of all Hans was leaving behind—his childhood, his youth, his father buried on a hillside out back, his mother a firmly entrenched Northeastern but curious to journey with him to revisit this vast country of ours, "America the Beautiful." His wife, Jennifer, and his two daughters, Maxine and Margot, having already flown out, were settling into their new lives on that distant coast.

As we swept down Interstate 684, the "spacious skies" opened over our heads, Hans was looking forward to the "shining sea" 3,000 miles away and a new life there. This was no little jaunt to lower Westchester or Manhattan. Going West on Interstate 287, as always under construction, we crossed our first big river, the mighty Hudson, glittering in the early morning sunshine. How many more rivers to cross? The Delaware would be next. That we know.

Soon we turned on to Interstate Route 80 West, our first unfamiliar road, racing along with anxious commuters in their business suits and ties and their button down noses. Giant tractor trailers whooshed by; Hans had to keep a strong hold on the steering wheel, so we would not blow off the road, a practice we had to maintain all the way.

The commuters vanished; presumably they were safely behind their desks. Soon brick-flat, over-built suburban New Jersey gave way to rolling hills and tall evergreens. The Pocanos? Not yet. That comes after the Delaware River, and the hills are bigger out there. Even this far north, the Delaware is a formidable river; one wonders how George Washington was able to throw a coin across the stream farther down.

Hans and Lizzie are going west.

Right after crossing the Delaware, Hans decided the dogs needed to stretch and pee, so he turned into a little cemetery, a perfect place to stop. Lizzie, the young, white Westie, was the Alpha dog. She led the way, followed slavishly by Wendel, a home-bred, half-Jack Russell-half Tibetan terrier. One of the best features of this trip was that Hans who is by nature decisive, made all the decisions: where we'd stop for gas, food, whatever. He was the Alpha person on that trip, and I was glad to have someone else making the decisions. The dogs limited our sleeping options to Motel 6 and such, places that welcomed dogs. Cheap and cheerful, they were fine places to lay our heads.

On the road again and I was at the wheel. Listening to IPods—sometimes his, sometimes mine—the hours passed quickly. I had not spent this much time with Hans since he left for college, so we had a lot to catch up on. Current events: breaking news—who is the most stupid—the Professor? The Police? The President? My husband, Max, would have called it "a storm in a water glass." The news was full of a recent event in Massachusetts; a white cop arrested a black man, Professor Henry Louis Gates, Jr. of Harvard for breaking into his own house. The Harvard professor was understandably irate, his genes still suffering from generations of prejudice and abuse. However, even in a democracy, cops are cops, and we agreed the only way to deal with them was with groveling apologies, and not a moment later I had to demonstrate just that. A cop pulled me over for speeding: 85 mph in a 70 mph speed zone. I explained we were driving West and I was not used to Hans's high-powered car, blah blah, blah, and guess what? Checking out my grey hair and wrinkles, he let me off with not even a warning. "Profiling" snorted Hans, as we drove away. "He would have thrown the book at me." "Just a perk for getting old," I answered and put the car on cruise control to avoid future infractions.

Speeding across the vast undulating state of Pennsylvania, we came upon a place we sort of knew, the town of Hazelton where, in the eighties, Max and his partners built a plant to make Chinese food pails, the little cartons with the wire handles, that they sold "like hot cakes" for decades. Clearly the product was good and the salesmen good at selling it. Their timing was also good. Many wives and mothers were working, so take out food picked up on the way home was an increasingly popular choice. When they sold the company in 1998, Foldpak had cornered over sixty percent of the market in the country. Not bad for a German who arrived in Brooklyn by freighter on a steamy 4th of July wearing a three-piece wool suit with two hundred dollars in his pocket.

What Hans and I didn't know was how far away Hazelton was from Bedford. Weather permitting, Max often used to fly his little plane out there and back in one day. That was easy . . . and fun too, for he loved to fly. What was not easy and not fun was when the weather was bad, and he had to drive. Never one to stay away in a motel when he could get home, Max would always drive out and back in one day. Neither Hans nor I had any idea how very long a drive that was, especially in inclement weather: rain, fog, sleet, snow. As it was, it had taken us four hours, speeding at 70 miles per hour on a sunny day in summertime. One more reason to admire and appreciate Dad, as if there weren't hundreds already. I don't ever remember his complaining about the long day, leaving before 6 am and arriving home often after midnight.

Finally, we put that wide state of Pennsylvania behind us, our first milestone, for now we were officially in the Middle West: Ohio. Admittedly, a Northeastern snob, I did not see much of interest for many miles across Ohio, Indiana, Illinois. Having not given it any thought ever, I vaguely assumed Indiana was west of Illinois. Wrong! Totally wrong.

As we dropped Interstate 80 in favor of Interstate 74 and finally Interstate 70, the truth sank in; Indiana is east of Illinois. Already I was appreciating Eisenhower's wonderful Interstate system. In his biography Michael Korda explained why Eisenhower was so adamant about building a proper road system across this boundless country of ours. Shortly after he graduated from West Point, he was commissioned to take a convoy across the country in early spring. The trip was a nightmare, and Eisenhower vowed that if he was ever in a position to do something about the problem, he would . . . and as President, he did. Clearly this vast country needed to be connected by more than country roads.

Despite numerous grumblings on talk shows about our crumbling infrastructure, we saw a lot of road repairs. On our journey we estimated five to ten percent of the highways we traveled were under repair, slow single lane travel for miles. Admittedly we saw very few major excavations for stretches of new highway. It was mostly patch, patch, patch, but at least someone is making an effort, and something is better than nothing.

The Midwest overwhelmed us with its infinite straight roads and flat, flat, flat land for miles and miles, punctuated too often by endless malls, fast food joints, "convenience stores" at the ubiquitous gas stations. It's no wonder the world is not enamored of us Americans; excesses are everywhere, most of them unnecessary.

Most visible are the obese, waddling in and out of the too-convenient eateries. If they settled in to eat there, you can bet they were not wolfing down salads. Not just chubby, not roly-poly, not pudgy, not stout, not hefty, not plump, certainly not buxom, they were simply fat. The men's bellies hung loose and floppy over their low belts; the women's ankles bulged over their shoes. We don't want to know what is hidden under their tent dresses; the children, of all ages, were just fat all over from their eyebrows to their toes squished into flip-flops. How did we get so decadent? The twenty-first century version of the Roman Empire at its worst.

After passing Indianapolis, (still east of Illinois; my geography is improving) and a full 800 miles along the trail west, we felt skinny and hungry, so we treated ourselves to a real dinner in a proper restaurant. Enough fast food joints, thank you. Then after being turned away half a dozen times, even by the seedy motels, because of the dogs, we fell into our beds, surrounded by those very dogs and their dirt and fleas. The lizard stayed in the car on his rock now cool because the car was turned off, but he survived. The next day we had to let him warm up before he could think about catching and eating his fifteen live crickets which we also had on board.

Missouri

The next morning the dogs woke us up early, ears pricked listening to our neighbors slamming doors and driving off to start their day. Hans took them for a walk while I jumped into the shower. We grabbed some coffee at the motel, and by 8 am we were on the road again with the sun at our backs. With Indianapolis well behind us, Interstate 70 ran straight and true across the 'unrememberable' Middle West, past towns I had to find on the map as I write this to refresh my memory: Terre Haute (Indiana), Effingham, Vandalia, Greenville, Highland, (all in Illinois) and finally St. Louis the gateway to the West, situated on the turbulent Mississippi River, fed mostly by the nearly—as-formidable Missouri. Well situated where those two mighty rivers merge, it was first a fur trading post named in honor of the French king, Louis XIV. River boats and later the railroad connected St. Louis to the world, and its towering stainless steel arch visible from almost anywhere in the city and along the Interstate reminds us that it is indeed the gateway to the West.

The only other time I had been to St. Louis was sometime in the '80's when I judged one of the most extravagant horse shows of my life, the B and B Horse Show, Busch and Baskowitz. St. Louis is Budweiser country.

Mr. August Busch, then in his 80's, and Bob Baskowitz, the number one Budweiser bottler nationwide, staged an event that exhibitors from all over the Midwest flocked to every year. The prize money was generous, and the trophies, sterling silver beer mugs and such.

Bob Baskowitz, ruddy-faced and looking prosperous, came straight from his bottling plant to pick us judges up at the airport in his red Rolls Royce convertible, setting the tone for the weekend. All week he drove us back and forth to the horse show and the various parties. We stayed in his "pool house," with its well-appointed bedrooms, its own sauna, and a heated pool, of course. The horse show began at a civilized hour every day, 9 am, not like our Northeastern horse shows that want the first horse in the ring at 8 am sharp. Breakfast was at 8 am at the newly-remodeled Baskowitz kitchen. It was all very grand.

We earned our keep, judging all day long, for there were many entries. The solicitous committee served a delicious lunch to us in the judges' box while the traditional team of eight Clydesdales performed. The show management kept everything running smoothly, so we were finished at 5 pm and could join the exhibitors for a beer, Budweiser, of course. All week long a giant tractor trailer, equipped with numerous beer spigots on both sides, kept everyone (but us judges!) cool under the broiling Missouri sun. We gladly waited until we were finished judging before sampling the beer, and did it ever taste good!

Then back to the pool house in the Rolls Royce to enjoy the sauna, the pool, and a shower before a full schedule of parties. One night we were invited to Mr. Busch's grand home. Imposing, heavy-set, and genial, he was the ultimate host at the head of a long, heavily laden table. Just then Bud Lite was the new thing, but he had no use for it.

Halfway through his first glass of beer, he filled the glass with water, saying:

"You want Bud Lite? Well, here it is. The great unwashed love it, and if I can't sell them what they should have, a nice, frosty Bud, I'll sell them what they want."

Words of a salesman, if ever I heard them. I took that bit of wisdom home, and if a client didn't buy the horse he should have, I sold him the one he wanted. It worked for me.

The most extravagant party was Saturday night when all the exhibitors, hundreds of them, were invited to the stable for a barbecue. The stable was a magnificent stone edifice built around a giant courtyard where the party was held. Elephants, giraffes, and other exotic animals stood by patiently as we petted and admired them. Dinner was shrimp cocktail, flown in "from the coast," and steak raised there in Missouri on the farm.

The farm itself, hundreds, probably thousands, of acres of rolling hills was home not only to the cattle but to dozens of Clydesdales, many big mares, and the foals were already over 16 hands high, the size of a real horse.

Exhausted on Sunday night after long days of judging and parties every night, we stepped from the breezy Rolls Royce, checks in hand, into the narrow tourist class airplane seats bound for the Northeast and ordinary life again. It was quite a weekend

While I was in St. Louis, Budweiser-land, judging the horse show, I was vaguely aware that a proxy fight was in progress, but I had no inkling how intense and far-reaching that battle was. In retrospect, one could say it was the beginning of the end of Budweiser as we knew it, and ultimately the end of Budweiser-USA which happened only recently when a foreign company bought our American icon. Having originally come from a Czech town, Budevoice, the beer known then as Bucavice, returned to European roots.

An avid horseman, August Busch, Sr. was a staunch supporter of our sport of show jumping. In the 1950's he helped our fledgling US Equestrian Team. When the US Cavalry was disbanded after World War II, he bought an extraordinary grey mare named Circus Rose, renamed her Miss Budweiser, and sent her to Helsinki for the Olympic Games in 1952. He was at the ingate when she jumped clear rounds and lead our U.S. team to the Bronze Medal. Since then his off-spring, all branches of the family, have been ardent riders, owners, and sponsors of our sport. They will always be riders and owners, but the question of sponsorship is bleak. The hundreds of thousands of dollars they poured into our major Grand Prix may be missing in the future. Finding another supporter like Budweiser is indeed unlikely.

When Interstate 70 veered off to the North we followed Interstate 44 from the northeast to the southwest across toward Oklahoma. What surprised us most about Missouri were the vineyards, miles and miles of them on both sides of the road.

"Whoever heard of Missouri wine?" we Northeastern snobs asked each other. "Is it any good? Or is it just glorified vinegar."

By late afternoon we decided to find out. Many of the vineyards have swell-looking centers with big signs inviting wayward travelers like ourselves to stop in and taste their wine. After passing about a half a dozen of these places, we decided to try one. After walking the dogs and checking the lizard, we went into a large, air-conditioned building whose walls were lined with rows and rows of wine. In the center was a rectangular counter behind which stood servers, college boys and girls enjoying a fun summer job. They set little, clear, plastic cups in front of each bottle for us to sample. Hot, dusty, and thirsty we would have savored any wine, no matter what. After sampling eight or ten wines and chatting with locals and travelers alike, we bought a couple of bottles and headed west. Woozy from the heat and the wine, we found a Starbucks and the caffeine revived us, so we could put a couple hundred miles on the odometer until we stopped for the night.

But before we called it a day, we passed another meaningful landmark. As we sped across the hot, dusty flatland south west of Missouri, past the town of Rolla, I reminded Hans that this was where Max did his basic training for six months when Uncle Sam slapped him in the Army soon after he got off the freighter in Brooklyn when he arrived from Germany in 1956. Despite the rigorous program, the ugly landscape, the insufferable heat, Max never lost sight of the American Dream. He loved this country, warts and all. For him there were plenty of warts in Missouri, and we were glad to by-pass the exit to the Fort Leonard Wood Military Reservation.

"Yeah," said Hans, "And this is where he got it in his head that it was bad to drink water, during the heat of the day. Only after sunset . . ." A bone of contention for years in our family, we never could persuade him to drink water until the sun set. He sweltered all those years mowing our fields. It was one of the very few things we argued about, more intensely as the boys grew stronger and Max frailer. Not drinking water all day long certainly was a bad idea, but he was more than a bit stubborn about it.

Our goal for day two was to put an additional 800 miles under our wheels before turning in for the night, so we could coast the last three days, covering five hundred miles each day and savoring the scenery and the flavor of the West. Somewhere near Oklahoma City we found a Pizza Hut and a motel that took dogs. It was late and we grabbed a quick bite before falling into bed.

The West

The next morning we woke up, glad that the West laid ahead of us, and we were eager to explore. A skimpy dinner the night before made us ravenous, so we joined the regulars, mostly construction workers and farmers in bib overalls at a nice old-fashioned breakfast joint across the street for bacon and eggs, toast and coffee. Tango, the lizard, was too cold to eat his designated fifteen live crickets, so we popped them back in the box with their friends 'til the next stop for gas when surely the temperature would be in the 80's and '90's, warm enough for him to think about breakfast. The dogs, on the other hand, gobbled up their chow, and again we were on the road by 8 am with the sun beaming behind us.

Our destination that day was Santa Fe, a mere five hundred miles away, where an old friend agreed to take us in for the night. We hoped to get there by mid-afternoon, so we could explore the city. Route 44 stretched clear and flat and inviting us as far as we could see. In Oklahoma City we picked up Route 40, another open highway, but more interesting to me was the winding, little two-lane blacktop road to our right. Sure enough, it was the famous Route 66, the Oakies road out of the dust bowl to prosperity in California. What an unpretentious little road it was to carry all those rosy dreams westward. Looking out the window of our comfortable air-conditioned car at the empty, dry landscape it was not hard to understand why the Oakies wanted something better, and it was easy to picture them—hot, dusty, exhausted—as they struggled westward with their families and few worldly possessions squeezed into their rusty, dilapidated vehicles. Ghosts of skinny, hollow-eyed children stared at us as we cruised along comfortably cooled by the droning air conditioner.

Hours later and miles farther down that straight and empty road across the desert, Hans decided we were ahead of schedule, and we had time for a side trip to Mádrid, pronounced Mádrid. A tiny village high in the hills north of Route 40, Mádrid is frozen in time; it is virtually a hippie town and has not changed since the '60's, according to Hans. He discovered it on one of his bicycle trips across the country. We turned off the highway and followed a narrow, little road up and up through the hills, admiring the huge, white clouds, crossing the deep blue sky.

In Mádrid there were no business suits and ties and button-down collars. The shabby village itself was indeed hippie land. Worn jeans and long hair framing gaunt faces were everywhere. We parked the car under a tree, let the dogs out to pee and have a drink of water, and found the bar Hans remembered. Seldom has a cold beer tasted so good as we sat on wobbly stools and exchanged pleasantries and philosophies with the locals. On our way out of town I reminded myself how glad I was Hans was making all the decisions on this trip; it would have been a shame to miss Mádrid.

Santa Fe

Santa Fe was as magical a place as I had remembered when I drove through with two college friends tin-canning around the country in 1959. Crowds were listening to music in the square in the center of town. We wandered around looking at the shops and the art exhibits in the streets. Glorious summer weather enhanced the magic as we sought out our friend Jay's home in a "development outside of town." It certainly did not feel like a development. Low adobe houses nestled among scrubby, little trees, and rolling hills hid one house from the next. Jovial Jay and his boisterous dogs greeted us enthusiastically and showed us around his home, suffused with Southwestern colors as the outdoors merged into the indoors. Adobe browns, and dark reds were everywhere. After another concert on the green and dinner in town we fell into bed, saturated with Santa Fe. It's no wonder when Hans and his family decided to "go West," Santa Fe was their first choice, but there were no good job offers, so they looked further and found San Diego.

Hans had decided our next stop would be Sedona, so we were in no rush to get started. It was only a mere 500 miles away, an easy day's driving by our standards. Having put 800 miles under our wheels two days in a row, we could coast to the coast which we did.

After a hearty breakfast with Jay on his sun-drenched patio, Hans fed Tango his fifteen lively crickets. We purposely left the car parked in the sun, so Tango would be warm enough to eat. He voraciously snapped up his hapless victims, we tossed our bags and the dogs into the car, thanked our jovial host and his boisterous dogs, and soon were "on the road again" south to Albuquerque. We resisted the temptations to visit the various pueblos along the way. After all, 500 miles is 500 miles, and this was no lazy sauntering tourist tour. In Albuquerque we picked up Interstate 40 again and sped along for hours past non-descript scenery, declining to visit the Navajo Nation Indian Reservation, a variety of missions, the New Mexico Museum of Mining and other points of interest. After we passed Gallup and got into Arizona, we were in desert country, flat and arid. The temperature outside our chilly car was 108°, and it looked that hot from where we sat. We gave the Painted Desert and the Petrified Forest a miss. Surely they have not changed much since I explored them in the '50's, and certainly no different from what Hans saw on one of his bicycle jaunts across the country. Been there, done that.

In Flagstaff we headed south on Interstate 17 (thank you, President Eisenhower, for your wonderful Interstates!) Those Interstates gave us the leisure to take a small country road, Alt 89 through increasingly majestic scenery. Tall mountains of red rocks and giant evergreens flanked both sides of the road for miles and miles. After racing mindlessly for hours on the Interstates, we were glad to saunter along and enjoy the breathtakingly beautiful world just outside our windows.

Sedona proved to be even more picturesque and charming than Hans had described. I'm glad he included it on our itinerary, for its quaint streets, shops, and homes were lovely. A favorite vacation destination for Westerners, the strict zoning laws have prevented it from becoming too "touristy." Natural beauty is treasured here and prevails still. Sedona also featured the nicest fleabag motel on the whole trip, an extra perk we had not counted on. Having snacked sporadically at convenience store/gas stations during the day as we were gassing up, draining the plumbing, walking the dogs, we were more than ready for a hearty dinner, which has become our habit on this journey. The motel people recommended a good restaurant nearby where we enjoyed the typical All-American dinner: steak, mashed potatoes, corn on the cob, salad. Perfect. We fell into our comfortable beds early and slept well until dawn.

Because there were dire reports on the radio about an accident with an oil spill on Interstate 10, just west of Phoenix, we opted to take back roads cross country through the mountains. Alt 89 looked like a short cut, but it was not, thanks to the winding roads and steep grades but it was a beautiful drive, so we had no regrets. On both sides of the road we were surrounded by tall, red rock mountains and giant evergreens, glorious weather and overwhelming scenery.

As we continued on the picturesque Alt 89, the next point of interest was Prescott, Arizona. Even as children, we appreciated the magical aura of that far-away place, and I was not disappointed. Less mountainous than Sedona, the town was similarly quaint and charming, with a slightly more Western aura. South of Prescott we passed between the Harquahala Mountains and finally picked up Interstate 10 in Quartzsize—wonderful name! Some of the fun of this trip is the names of the places that run the gamut from unpronounceable Indian names like the mountain ranges we just passed to the banal and amusing Quartzsize.

Soon we crossed our last great river, the mighty Colorado River that nourishes much of the West. At last we were in California and close to our destination. We cut south on 78 through some wine country where we stopped and sampled various wines at a vineyard owned by friends of friends.

As we turned south on Route 5, the local Interstate, Hans called his girls and, sure enough they were at the beach in Cardiff. We drove directly to the ocean, and after excited greetings and hugging, Hans plunged into the Pacific Ocean. He had arrived, and I will hold in my heart until I see them again and forever after the picture of the four of them standing together with the two dogs in front of the mighty Pacific Ocean. The trip west was, is, and probably will be the inevitable part of our culture as a family and as a nation. Life is indeed about leaving and moving on as well as being left and moving on.

"Go West, Young Man, Go West."
They have gone west: my son Hans;
his wife, Jennifer, daughters, Maxine and Margot, and the dogs,
Lizzie and Wendel.

Edwards Brothers, Inc.
Thorofare, NJ USA
December 20, 2011